LIVE AWARE, NOT IN FEAR

LIVE AWARE, NOT IN FEAR

The 411 After 9-11

A Book for Teens

Donna K. Wells, M.Ed., M.P.A.
Bruce C. Morris, J.D.

HCI TEENS™

Health Communications, Inc.
Deerfield Beach, Florida

www.hci-online.com

**Cataloging-in-Publication Data
is on file with the Library of Congress.**

©2002 Donna K. Wells and Bruce C. Morris
ISBN 0-7573-0013-8

HCI Teens, its Logos and Marks are trademarks of Health Communications, Inc.

Publisher: Health Communications, Inc.
            3201 S.W. 15th Street
            Deerfield Beach, FL 33442-8190

Cover design by Lisa Camp
Inside book design by Lawna Patterson Oldfield

To my Bean and my Bug,
stay safe.
I love you, Mom

—Donna

To all the precious children, including mine,
who are our future and who
make it all worthwhile.

—Bruce

In memory of all those who have
laid down their lives for us, and in honor of
those who roll out and put it all on the line
every day—dedicated public safety, health
and military professionals everywhere.

And thanks to you, Michael.

Contents

Acknowledgments

We acknowledge, with gratitude and appreciation, the assistance and cooperation provided by an outstanding family of professionals at Health Communications, Inc. From our editors, Christine Belleris, Lisa Drucker and Susan Tobias; to the marketing, public relations and sales teams, including Kelly Maragni, Kim Weiss and Lori Golden; to the designers and artists, including Larissa Hise Henoch, Lisa Camp and Lawna Patterson Oldfield; to layout, copy and print specialists; to the big guys, Peter Vegso and Tom Sand: Thank you for your service, faith and support.

And to our colleagues in the Commonwealth of

Virginia, the Domestic Preparedness Working Group, the Governor's Preparedness and Security Panel, and our fellow state employees who do so much every day to keep Virginia safe and secure: You are the best; we are honored to be among you.

A special tribute goes to the late Richard L. Piermarini, friend and photographer (forensic and portrait) extraordinaire—you are missed.

Introduction

Panic. Fear. Apprehension. Disbelief. Confusion.

Which of these did you feel on September 11? Or what combination? What are you feeling now?

September 11, 2001, has been called "the day the world changed," and it certainly did. Nothing's quite the same as it was before that day. We've entered a war on terrorism. The ways we work, travel, shop, communicate—live—have been altered. The media bombards us, first with reassurances that life can return to normal, then with news of the latest biomedical scare, bomb threat or security breach. It's easy to see how anyone might get confused.

It may seem like an adult's world now with adults in charge, but soon it will be your turn. You know you need to be informed and want to be, but, admit it, you're not sure you want to be responsible. It might be easier to play it safe and stay stuck in limbo—in some in-between stage where you don't have to act or make the decisions.

But you do need to know as much as you can about what's going on and how to react to events. You need to be informed so you can make responsible decisions. Much of what we all do now will shape the future—your future.

This book is about information. The real deal. Not to scare you with hype or hysteria. Not to dumb anything down. Just the truth. Presenting, in a readable format, some basics and essentials about what has been called our "new normalcy." Ours is a complicated world, and it always has been. Now we are facing unprecedented challenges to our safety and security. Our values and way of life are the objects of terrorists' hate and destruction. Working together, we can confront these threats.

Times are different, sure, but not unmanageably so. Decisions and adjustments can be made. You are stronger and better informed than many generations before you.

With sound information, you will make rational decisions and take appropriate actions. You will, because you must.

And when you do, you will learn to live aware, not in fear.

1

Home of the Brave

RISK SCENARIO— WHAT WOULD YOU DO?

You recall your parents talking about a *Peanuts* cartoon from their childhoods where Charlie Brown tells Linus, "No problem is so big it cannot be run away from." You recall that and smile, but only faintly. All the talk of terrorism, biological agents, epidemics, explosions and cyber crime is making you crazy. And it is making you afraid. You aren't afraid of an attack hurting you or someone about whom you care so much as you are afraid of not knowing what to do, not knowing how to respond, not knowing whether you will measure up.

1

Will you be able to take care of yourself and those around you? What are the things you should do to be prepared? What must you know that you have no idea about now?

LIFE BEFORE 9-11 WAS SO SIMPLE. OR SO IT SEEMED.

Last night you and your buddies gathered at Chip's house after the game, after the dance. It was the usual Friday night—go to the game, go to the dance, hang out—except that it wasn't. No Friday night has been usual or the same this fall. This year was supposed to be special. This year was supposed to be *the* year—fun, exciting, adventurous. You in control. In command, taking charge. Now it seems like nothing about your life is in your control. Your folks demand to know where you are and what you are doing constantly. The media, even *Imus in the Morning* and your two favorite radio stations, pound you with the horrors of the attacks, the evil threat of terrorism. Your mom and dad seem different—preoccupied, worried. Teachers and coaches, the same. You're sick of it all. You just want things to go back to the way they were.

What did you do to deserve this? Why now?

It's not that you really are that selfish. Not that you don't care about what has happened or what could occur. You just don't know what to do. No one is telling you much generally about what is going on in the country or your community. And no one is telling you anything specific about what you can or should do to help. You feel like you are lost, drifting around in a sea of confusion, drowning in the unknown.

Roger called this morning and wants you to go with him to visit his older brother, Jason, a junior at State. Jason had helped organize a protest rally at the school. Hundreds of students had signed petitions against the bombings of Afghanistan and the escalation of the war on terrorism to other parts of the world. Thousands of people were expected to show up for the rally on the quad. It would be a way to get involved, to feel a part of something, anything. At least you would be getting some information, some direction. You need to get motivated, to take some action. What better way to act than to protest a war you don't really understand anyway, right? Who is for war?

But you didn't say "yes." And you didn't say "no."

Geez, you feel hopeless. You can't even decide a simple question of how to spend a Saturday. You want to learn more about what is going on. Still, joining a protest rally doesn't seem right. Not yet anyway. You don't know if you really believe the war is wrong.

You aren't in favor of war or killing, but someone killed thousands of innocent Americans and hundreds of people from other countries in the 9-11 attacks. Those victims weren't soldiers at war. They were businessmen and -women. Police officers, firefighters and medics. Moms and dads, sisters and brothers, sons and daughters. None of them picked the fight, and not one of them expected to be killed by a terrorist that day. Isn't this a matter now of kill or be killed? Isn't that what the politicians and generals say? Don't we have the right to avenge their deaths, to retaliate? Isn't the United States entitled, no, required, to defend herself and prevent more innocent citizens and visitors from being killed at the hands of fanatics and zealots? Aren't these attackers criminals, not crusaders?

Protesting action you truly oppose is one thing, but getting involved for the sake of getting involved because you are afraid and don't understand is another. Isn't that a bit misguided? And doesn't it cut against how you were raised, what you've been taught, and what you do believe in?

Before you lend support or opposition, don't you need to learn more and decide for yourself? Do you have a good basis for any decision now? If you are honest with yourself, isn't it the fear thing that is bothering you the most? You remember the quote of President Franklin D. Roosevelt, who in his first inaugural address in 1933 said to the American people, ". . . the only thing we have to fear is fear itself."

You don't want to be afraid. You certainly don't want to be moved to action by fear of the unknown.

The phone is ringing. Roger wants an answer.

How Much Do You Know?

1. When was the first time the United States declared war under the Constitution?

    a. 1961   c. 1812

    b. 1941   d. 1776

2. True or False: Only the president can declare war.

3. True or False: Until the 1960s, Americans never protested U.S. military action.

4. A declaration of war by the United States requires:

a. a kick-ass president

b. action by Congress

c. consent of the American people

d. nerves of steel

e. complete disregard for human life

5. True or False: The primary goal of terrorism is to induce fear and terror.

6. Dealing with our fears requires:

a. knowledge   d. support

b. preparation   e. all of the above

c. strategy   f. none of the above

7. True or False: There is very little an individual citizen can do to prepare for terrorism and deal with fear.

8. True or False: Only people directly injured in a terrorist attack suffer any harm.

9. In dealing with terrorism and the possibility of future attacks, it is important for our governmental leaders to:

a. provide timely information

b. be truthful

c. use the media (television, radio, newspapers)

d. balance what we need to know against threats to the military and law enforcement if too much is said too soon

e. all of the above

10. Many Americans did not fully appreciate our soldiers, sailors, marines, airmen, police, fire and rescue workers until:

a. September 11, 2001

b. the news media told them to do so

c. they became a victim of an attack personally

d. a and c

Answers can be found at the end of this chapter.

MYTH VS. FACT

Expecting the Worst

The oldest and strongest emotion of mankind is fear, and the oldest and strongest kind of fear is fear of the unknown.

H. P. Lovecraft

The Myth: There are terrorists everywhere in our country. Every citizen and visitor in our land is at risk because there is a threat around every corner. We are at war with an unknown, unseen enemy and the chances are great that many of us will become victims. This "fact" will instill uncontrollable fear in most of us, and there is very little we can do to manage our fear. We should all find a cave and hide.

Understanding the Rest

One ought never to turn one's back on a threatened danger and try to run away from it. If you do that, you will double the danger. But, if you meet it promptly and

without flinching, you will reduce the danger by half.
Never run away from anything. Never!

Winston Churchill

The Truth: Yes, our great nation is now at war against an enemy far different from those we have faced in the past. For the first time in a very long time, we are fighting this enemy on our own soil, as well as overseas. It is an unconventional war against an unusual enemy. Much about the why of what happened on September 11, 2001, and since that day is unknown. Much about what will happen next—tomorrow, next week, next month—is unknown. Not knowing is often what scares many of us the most. But there is much you can do to deal with our country's challenges and your fears, and to help others to do so, too.

You can be proactive at this time of challenge. You can learn to assess your threats and vulnerabilities, so you can reduce your risk and your stress. There is absolutely no reason for you to feel like a victim or become one. Although it is true that you cannot ensure your total safety 100 percent of the time, that was the case before September 11, 2001, as well. And the fact remains that you are at greater risk from routine dangers such as driving or riding in a car and household accidents than you are from attack by a terrorist. So get a grip. And be proactive—for yourself and others.

IGNORANCE IS NOT BLISS

- The threat of a terrorist attack to you, your home and family, your school and workplace is extremely small, but not nonexistent.
- Certain areas of the country and certain places within communities are generally at higher risk than others. For example, large metropolitan areas, and places such as malls and stadiums where large groups gather, generally are more attractive to terrorists seeking a great impact on people's lives. Federal buildings, financial institutions, power plants, bridges, tunnels and dams are among the physical structures in any community that may, depending upon the intelligence information

available to law enforcement and military agents, be possible targets at a given time.

- You are safer at home than anywhere else, but your school is very safe, also. You still need to be informed and prepared to react, wherever you are.

- Law enforcement, governmental officials and the news media will do their best to keep you informed, but cannot always help those who do not help themselves. You should make it your business to stay close to the news business: newspapers, radio, TV and the Internet.

- Your federal, state and local leaders, and public safety and health officials know more and are doing more than you realize to protect you and promote your safety and health. At times, telling you everything they know jeopardizes their efforts and puts lives in danger.

- Our country, diplomatically and militarily, is doing more than you realize to defeat terrorism and keep you safe. At times, telling you what they are doing, before or while they are doing it, jeopardizes their efforts and puts lives in danger.

UNFAMILIAR, NOT UNCHARTED

1. Why is so much attention being given to terrorism and terrorists? Terrorism isn't new to our country, is it?

Terrorism and terrorists are not a new threat to our country, but the horrific attacks of 9-11 and their dreadful consequences are new to us. Never before have so many American and foreign citizens, the majority nonmilitary personnel, been killed and injured in a single series of attacks in a single day on American soil.

2. What do terrorists target and why?

The purposes of terrorism include instilling fear and terror in people affected through an act of significant impact calculated to disrupt life, health, safety, communication, commerce and government, and undermining citizens' confidence in the ability of government to respond to and recover from the attack, as well as restore some sense of normalcy. Terrorists target people, places, structures and events they believe will maximize their impact and instill the greatest terror.

3. What does that mean for the average teen's everyday life?

The "new war" and the "new reality" are bringing forth old themes of loyalty, patriotism, duty, honor and service among all people, teens and others. Young people are responding to the challenges their country is facing with a new sense of obligation. Recruitment by military branches is high, as is interest among college students in public-service careers. The president of Harvard recently called a career in the military "a noble calling," and many universities are considering reinstating the Reserve Officers' Training Corps (ROTC) programs to their campuses, some at the request of students. For many teenagers, their pride in their country is being reinforced. For some, it means changing attitudes, increasing awareness and even changing some behaviors—either to satisfy their parents or to satisfy their own sense of responsibility.

4. How can the psychological consequences of terrorism, among them fear and stress, be managed best?

There are four psychological keys that mirror emergency management responses:

Preparedness: Leaders must inform us about practical steps we can take to prepare for and respond to acts of terrorism.

Informed Mitigation: Leaders must provide as much information as possible about the situation without jeopardizing lives or the missions of law enforcement and the military.

Stress Response: Healthcare experts must furnish advice and modalities for dealing with the fear and other emotions—worry, hate, dread—that result from terrorists' acts and our war on terrorism, and we should not hesitate to seek professional services when needed.

Support and Recovery: We need to provide back-up and sustenance for one another and seek the help of others when we need it.

THE COURAGE TO UNDERSTAND

Our strength is often composed of the weakness we're damned if we're going to show.

Mignon McLaughlin

1. What are your safety concerns about your community?

_____

_____

_____

_____

2. What are your greatest concerns about your immediate surroundings?

_____

_____

_____

_____

3. Is your community at higher risk, and how should that impact your family's plans and behaviors?

_____

_____

_____

_____

4. What kind of contingency plan does your family have in case something should happen in your city?

_____

_____

_____

_____

5. If your city were to be evacuated, where would you go?

_____

_____

_____

_____

6. What would you do if your parents were out of town and there was an emergency evacuation of your area?

_____

_____

_____

_____

7. Given a limited time to evacuate, what personal items (aside from necessities like food and water) would you take with you?

_____

_____

_____

_____

8. If there were a terrorist attack on your city, how do you think the people would react? Would they be orderly or panicked? How would you react?

_____

_____

_____

_____

9. In what ways has your day-to-day routine changed since September 11, 2001? How do you think it will continue to change?

_____

_____

_____

_____

10. In what ways can you do more to help your family, friends and country?

_____

_____

_____

_____

DON'T JUST SIT THERE

You don't get to choose how you're going to die or when. You can only decide how you're going to live today.

Joan Baez

1. Read! Newspapers, weekly newsmagazines and the Internet provide tons of helpful facts and advice to keep you up-to-date on what is happening. No, everything written isn't the gospel, but balancing what you read in different sources can help you form your own opinions and engage in healthy debate with others.

2. Observe! Yes, watching the news and TV newsmagazine programs can be helpful to expanding your knowledge base (but they are no substitute for reading). It is also critically important to be more observant than you have been about the world around you. Notice things. Only by being more cognizant of the routine and mundane in the world can you be alert to the unusual that may pose a threat to your safety. For example, if you are aware of the

cars on your street that belong to neighbors or travel back and forth routinely, then you will notice an out-of-place vehicle. The chances are against something strange presenting a challenge to your safety, of course, but if any situation is alarming enough to cause you concern, it is sufficient to report to your police department or sheriff's office. Remember: Law enforcement officials, too, would rather be proactive than reactionary.

3. Be alert and aware! Take notice of any situation or condition anywhere—at home, at school, at the mall or work, anywhere in your community, along your travels—that creates concern about safety or presents a safety challenge. Reading and informing yourself will help you recognize possible threats and know what to do to react to them. If you have any question about reporting something to officials in your community, do so. What's the worst that will happen? They will investigate, and it will most likely turn out to be nothing. You may feel foolish, but you shouldn't.

4. Recognize and embrace the fact that the actual threat of terrorism against yourself and your family

is incredibly, overwhelmingly small. And you can do much to reduce the threat further. Keep yourself informed. Avoid situations that don't "feel right." If it makes you uncomfortable for any reason to be in a given place at a given time, avoid it if you can. You can't use this as an excuse to skip school (you are safer there than anywhere else except home), but if you don't feel like hanging out among large groups of people at the mall or theater, then don't. You have control of your life (subject to parents' restrictions, of course).

5. Know what the real-life risk scenarios are in your world. From time to time, law enforcement or other governmental officials may inform us that certain activities or places are at a higher risk or greater threat level. When that happens, pay attention. If it means you avoid the mall, skip a concert, don't ride your jet ski on the lake near the power plant or your dirt bike in the woods near the reservoir, so be it. Find something else to do. Listen to a CD. Play a video game. Read! Be aware of your proximity to places and situations that may be identified as targets. If you live near a nuclear

power plant or in a flood plain, disaster plans and evacuation routes are probably already known to you. The rest of us need to be just as aware of our surroundings and response capabilities.

6. Be a good citizen and a responsible family member. Whether you accept a "you are your brother's keeper" role or not, accept that we all have some responsibility to look out for one another. If someone else, known or unknown to you, became aware of a threat to your safety, you would certainly want (expect) them to notify you. Do the same for others. It is particularly important now that we look out for those close to us. Keep tabs on family members, especially younger brothers and sisters.

7. Know the necessities of and help prepare a family disaster plan, a family escape plan and "go bags." Don't forget pets. All members of every family should know what to do and where to go if safety challenges make it necessary to evacuate your community. Your escape route should be well-planned and well-known. Know where to meet, other than home, if you get split up or begin your evacuation from different points, such as work and school. For

example, plan to meet at the community center, neighborhood clubhouse or Uncle Fred's house. Have a footlocker or large plastic container packed and ready to go with enough food and water for a minimum of three to five days. Keep camping gear handy and ready to throw in a car. Have a portable radio and spare batteries handy, as well as a family first-aid kit. Prepare a personal "go bag" with a change of clothes, toiletries and outerwear that you can grab in a hurry.

8. Know how to use technology to your maximum advantage. From TV, radio and the Internet to pagers, cell phones and family radios (walkie-talkies), today's technology can improve your disaster response and safety insurance capabilities. Buy what you can afford, and know how to use what you buy. Keep devices fully charged and spare batteries handy.

9. Know yourself, your reactions and how to manage your stress and fear. Your mental health is as important to your survival as your physical well-being and a lot more likely to be "attacked." Although the likelihood that you will be physically assaulted by

a terrorist is extremely remote, the possibility that you might suffer some form of stress, mental and/or emotional strain, unless you are made of stone or have ice water in your veins, is fairly high. These are challenging times for all of us. Don't be afraid to talk to others about your concerns or reluctant to seek help from professional caregivers. Whether you are losing sleep or weight as a result of fear and concern, you should be tuned in to your biological signals and take appropriate action. Your mental health is important and can impact your physical fitness. Both can influence your ability to react to, respond to and recover from safety challenges.

10. Take pride in what you and your family are doing to stay safe and well and look after one another. Be proud of what your country is doing to defeat terrorism and make the world safer. Show your support by displaying the flag.

WHAT ARE THE CHANCES?

Your level of threat can be assessed by determining the probability—or likelihood—of a particular risk factor affecting you, and the level of impact—or consequence—of that threat. For example, your likelihood of being involved in a commercial jet crash is fairly low, but the consequences of such a crash are high. Conversely, your likelihood of being involved in a car crash during your lifetime is high, but the consequences are relatively low. A matrix of this example would look like this.

| | CONSEQUENCES | |
	LOW	HIGH
LIKELIHOOD HIGH	car crash	
LOW		plane crash

Based on what you know about your lifestyle, your community, current threats you may face and what you have learned, rate the likelihood and the consequence of each of the following vulnerabilities. Then write the number of that vulnerability in the appropriate box on the matrix provided at the end of this chapter to assess your level of risk from the vulnerabilities listed. You are building a matrix that will include all the threats in this book.

VULNERABILITIES

1. Location of home
2. Type of housing
3. Proximity to major city
4. Being separated from family members

	CONSEQUENCES	
	LOW	HIGH
HIGH		
LOW		

LIKELIHOOD

Answers: How Much Do You Know?

1. c • 2. F • 3. F • 4. b • 5. T • 6. e • 7. F • 8. F • 9. e • 10. d

2

Worried Sick

RISK SCENARIO—
WHAT WOULD YOU DO?

It's late—long after midnight on Friday night. Your parents are asleep. You're online, chatting with friends. Suddenly, the phone rings. You grab it before Caller ID registers, hoping you get it before your dad wakes up. He's not fond of late-night calls.

On the line is your best friend, Jessica, and she sounds terrible. Right away, that worries you. Jessica's parents are out of town for the weekend, so you know she's home alone. She seems to be having trouble breathing, and she says she can't stand up. She has a bad headache, and she's running a fever. Most disturbing, she sounds scared.

"I think I may have anthrax," she whispers hoarsely. "I'm having trouble breathing. And I ache all over, and my head hurts."

"I'll come over and get you," you offer.

"No!" Her attempt at a scream comes out as barely a whisper. "Do you want to get it, too?"

"Jess," you reply soothingly, "there haven't been any anthrax threats here. You probably just have the flu. But, either way, you shouldn't be alone."

"You don't understand," she whispers. "Last week, I got a belated birthday card from my aunt and uncle. The day I opened it, Uncle Josh called me and told me not to open the card because it had been mailed from a post office that tested positive for anthrax the next day. I've tried to reach my parents, but they aren't at the hotel. I am so scared!"

Jess can be a little emotional sometimes. And, logically, you think she probably just has the flu. You've heard a lot about anthrax, of course, and you sort of remember that the symptoms can match those of the flu, but what if it is anthrax? Could it be? What do you do?

How Much Do You Know?

1. When was germ warfare first used?

    a. during the Vietnam War

    b. during World War II

    c. during World War I

    d. hundreds and hundreds of years ago

2. Tularemia, a potential biological weapon, is also known as:

    a. black death   c. shingles

    b. rabbit fever   d. smallpox

3. The death rate for smallpox is:

    a. 100%   c. 50%

    b. 70%   d. 30%

4. What are the different kinds of anthrax infection?

    a. inhalation   d. all of the above

    b. cutaneous   e. only a & b

    c. intestinal

5. True or False: Botulism is highly contagious.

6. Smallpox:

   a. cannot spread in areas where the temperature remains below freezing

   b. does not spread during winter months

   c. doesn't spread in temperatures above 90°F

   d. can spread in any climate or season

7. True or False: The plague can only be introduced into an area through fleas and rats.

8. You were not given a smallpox vaccine as a child because:

   a. there wasn't enough of a supply to vaccinate everyone

   b. it caused severe reactions in nearly 20% of those vaccinated

   c. vaccination was too costly

   d. smallpox had been considered an eradicated disease

9. How many countries have access to smallpox stockpiles?

   a. two   c. six

   b. three   d. no one knows

10. *The death rate for the plague is nearly:*

    a. 100%   *c. 50%*

    b. 75%   *d. 30%*

Answers can be found at the end of this chapter.

MYTH VS. FACT

Expecting the Worst

How can such episodes of such savage cruelty happen? The heart of man is an abyss out of which sometimes emerge plots of unspeakable ferocity capable of over-turning in an instant the tranquil and productive life of a people.

Pope John Paul II
September 2001

The Myth: One germ, released in several locations across the United States, would spread so rapidly that it would soon overtake the health-care system and the entire population would be at grave risk.

The anthrax outbreak on the heels of the terrorist events of September 11, 2001, caught everyone by surprise, including law-enforcement officials, health specialists and our government leaders. Even though we have had clues in the past, we have not wanted to accept the fact that biological terrorism on U.S. soil is a distinct threat. At first, officials thought that just a few individuals might have been exposed to anthrax and that only one or two would contract it. Within days, they realized how widespread the effects of the attack actually were.

Now, many fear that the Western world is at risk for an even greater biological attack that could kill thousands or even millions. The key is to understand what germs are considered biological threats, what their availability is and just how lethal they can be.

Understanding the Rest

Terrorist attacks can shake the foundation of our biggest buildings, but they cannot touch the foundation of America. These acts shatter steel, but they cannot dent the steel of American resolve.

President George W. Bush

The Truth: Prior to the terrorist events of September 11, 2001, if someone had asked you about anthrax, you might have thought it was a type of detergent, a rock band or, perhaps, a chemical. Now you know more about this germ than your parents ever believed you would have to know. But what about other organisms terrorists might use against us? How potent are they? How easily can they be acquired? Who already has them? What can we do to prevent outbreaks?

In addition to anthrax, the most likely bioterrorism weapons include the plague, botulism, tularemia and smallpox. Although they vary in their potential for use, fatality rate and availability, each demands quick diagnosis. Fortunately, government health experts now recognize the need to address these risks.

The early symptoms of inhaled anthrax mirror those of the flu, including fever, headache and general muscle soreness. There are also differences. Anthrax causes a dry cough and is not accompanied by a runny nose.

More common is cutaneous anthrax, which is caused by anthrax bacteria penetrating the skin through a cut or abrasion. At first, the infection resembles a bug bite, but within a few days, it develops into a dark blister. The third way anthrax enters the body is when a person eats food contaminated with the germ. Ingesting anthrax this way may cause intestinal anthrax. Those symptoms include vomiting (including vomiting of blood) and fever, followed by severe abdominal pain and diarrhea. Anthrax can be treated successfully with antibiotics if the infection is caught early.

Botulism is exceptionally poisonous and can be spread through the air or in food. Initial symptoms include blurred vision and slurred speech, followed by paralysis. The paralysis eventually reaches the respiratory system, shutting down the lungs. Using botulism as a terrorist agent has been tried before. Warheads containing anthrax and botulism toxins were discovered in Iraq by United Nations inspectors in the mid-1990s. They had not been successfully deployed.

Smallpox, a highly contagious viral disease, can spread quickly when infected individuals sneeze or cough. In the early 1900s, smallpox reached epidemic proportions throughout the world. All children in the United States and many across the world were vaccinated against the disease. The last known case of smallpox was in 1977, and by 1980, the World Health Organization declared that the disease had been eradicated. But two known stockpiles were kept, and now it is feared that additional virus samples exist in at least three other countries. There are several types of smallpox infection, which cause severe pain and misery and result in death.

The plague is a bacterium carried by rodents and fleas and can survive in most areas of the world. Small stores of the plague are kept in laboratories and research facilities. Until 1996, such samples were fairly easy to acquire. That year, Larry Wayne Harris, a student at Ohio State University, was able to obtain three vials of the plague bacterium by using counterfeit university letterhead. Harris was considered to be a white supremacist. He was actually carrying the bacteria in his car when he was arrested.

In addition to biological agents that can be used against us, artificially engineered chemical agents have also been developed and pose a threat to us. In 1995, Aum Shinrikyo, a Japanese cult, released sarin, a chemical nerve gas, in a Tokyo subway, killing a dozen people and injuring hundreds. Sarin is usually inhaled, but can also penetrate through the skin. There are antidotes available for certain chemical nerve agents that paralyze the respiratory system.

In addition to sarin, the most likely chemical weapons available today include mustard gas, VX and tabun. Mustard gas can be ingested, inhaled or taken in through the skin. Unlike sarin, it is a blistering agent and there is no known treatment for it. Exposure to deadly mustard gas causes extensive damage to a person's respiratory system. VX is another nerve gas that can enter the body through the skin and is particularly dangerous because it can remain viable for long periods of time. Tabun is the least lethal of the most available chemical weapons and the easiest to produce.

In 1984, an accidental leak at a Union Carbide plant in Bhopal, India killed three thousand people and injured thousands more. While that event was accidental, one concern now is whether the chemical plants in this country are vulnerable to attack. In many places, there are highly hazardous, toxic materials located close to or even inside city limits. At some facilities, no background checks have been conducted on personnel in the plants. Others are adjacent to major highways and/or rail lines.

Still others receive unscheduled deliveries, all of which increase their risk of attack.

Potential terrorists who want to use germ warfare would have to be experienced in the development and transfer of biological agents. The same individuals, if willing to use a chemical attack, might only have to use one of our own facilities as the target.

Studies conducted by the U.S. Environmental Protection Agency (EPA) have indicated that hundreds of facilities in the nation, if attacked, could spread toxic fumes for miles across the landscape. In worst case scenarios, hundreds or even thousands of innocent citizens could be killed.

Another cause for concern is that hazardous materials are also regularly transported around the country by truck and by rail. If one of these transports were attacked, it would also provide a significant chemical threat to communities. In the wake of the September 11, 2001, attacks, many commercial procedures have undergone review and revision, making the chances of a successful attack less likely.

IGNORANCE IS NOT BLISS

All of these agents are dangerous to the public. Consider the following facts:

- The plague and smallpox are extremely contagious. While anthrax, botulism and tularemia are not transmitted from person to person, they can be transmitted environmentally.

- The death rate for the plague is nearly 100 percent, although that can be cut in half if antibiotics are given immediately after the first symptoms begin. Symptoms appear within a week of exposure to the germ, and death occurs rapidly after that—usually within a few days.

- The fatality rate for smallpox is about one in three. Symptoms appear in seven to seventeen days, and death usually follows in about two weeks. The vaccine, if available, is 100 percent effective in preventing the disease, but it is not without risk. Historically, about two out of every million vaccinated individuals suffered brain injury and death from the vaccine. If we had been vaccinating children during the last twenty years, it is believed about two hundred of them would have died from the vaccination. U.S. laboratories are now producing large quantities of smallpox vaccines that are being stored ("stock-piled") for emergency use, if needed.

• The fatality rate for tularemia, also known as rabbit fever, is about one in eight. The symptoms occur within five days and include fever and chills, fatigue, swollen lymph nodes and pneumonia. Relatively speaking, this is the least lethal of the potential warfare germs, and it can be treated with antibiotics.

• Many people worry about being poisoned through city or county water systems, but the fact is, most are fairly safe. Public water systems treat their supply with various benign chemical agents, which keep us safe from terrorist chemical/biological attacks.

• Even our domestic food supply is relatively safe from large-scale attack, but that doesn't mean we aren't at risk. We are at greater risk for foods that come into the United States from other countries, so it is important to learn the source of your foods. When your parents were kids, they probably didn't have the wide variety of fresh fruits and vegetables all year that you enjoy, because such foods, for the average American, weren't regularly imported from other countries. Today, they are. Still, most grocery stores can tell you if a particular food was grown in this country or came in from another.

UNFAMILIAR, NOT UNCHARTED

1. Where did these diseases come from?

Most are naturally occurring germs. Anthrax, for example, was first identified more than one hundred years ago, in 1876, and can survive naturally in the soil for years. Many of these chemicals and germs have been used throughout history in warfare. Hundreds of years ago, warriors spread the plague by throwing infected corpses into the cities they sought to overtake. Many believe that the smallpox outbreak among Native Americans in the mid-1700s was caused deliberately by the English because the Indians had been supporting the French. Much more recently, in 1984, 750 people in a town in Oregon were infected with salmonella in a deliberate attack by Bagwan Shree Rajneesh and his followers. Overall, attacks are rare and usually limited in scope.

2. Why aren't we vaccinated against all of them?

Vaccines can be expensive, and they often have significant side effects. Medical specialists and government leaders usually decide when vaccines are required.

3. But, even if the cost and the risks are high, isn't the threat even higher?

Traditionally, the risks were higher than the threat. Now that we know there are others who have and will use biological weapons against the public, government leaders are reconsidering current practices. Efforts to develop safe vaccines and treatments for the known germs of bioterrorism are ongoing.

4. If I choose to accept the risk and the cost, can I get vaccinated against these diseases?

Americans were routinely vaccinated against smallpox until the early 1970s. At that time, because the disease had been eradicated worldwide, medical specialists decided it was no longer necessary to vaccinate everyone, especially since there was a small, but severe, health risk from the vaccination.

In the case of the plague, a vaccine was available until 1998 to military personnel, lab workers and others at high risk of infection. A limited supply of the anthrax vaccine is available for military personnel, lab researchers, veterinarians and others who are at significant risk. Similarly, a vaccine is available for those at high risk of tularemia infection, but that supply is also limited. A botulism vaccine was abandoned years ago by the U.S. military; a new, experimental one is now available on a limited basis.

5. How great is the risk today?

The anthrax attack, like the destruction of the World Trade Center and the attack on the Pentagon, served as a wake-up call for the government. It forced the medical community and our political leaders to focus on this threat and take immediate steps. Now they are working to ensure that these diseases can be prevented, when possible, or detected in the earliest stages and treated.

6. If these germs are so deadly, how do terrorists get them?

Many commercial and scientific labs keep dangerous agents on hand for research purposes. In some cases, they can be purchased or simply stolen. Smallpox was completely eradicated except for two caches of the bacteria—one in the United States at the Centers for Disease Control and Prevention (CDC) and one in Russia. Some fear that at least part of the Russian sample has been stolen or sold, possibly to terrorists.

7. Why are some of these germs so widely available?

In part, because we kept believing that they would be used primarily for research and medical purposes, not for warfare. Therefore, our government did not keep a detailed inventory of supplies in government or private labs. In 1999, a federal bill was introduced that would have greatly increased controls on the exchange and production of such organisms, but the legislation died when it was opposed by many of our own universities.

8. How easy is it to "manufacture" these germs?

In many cases, it's quite easy. If someone has access to a supply, a sample of it can often be taken out of a facility in a test tube or petri dish and then replicated elsewhere. And, if an individual isn't sure how to do it, the directions are often available on the Internet or in libraries. On the other hand, once manufactured, these agents are difficult to unleash.

9. Should my family buy gas masks?

The chances are that the mask you could buy for use in the case of a chemical attack would do little good. Many gases are odorless and colorless, so unless you wear a mask constantly, they could get to you before you get to your mask. Also, many of the masks being sold are surplus. They may have air filters that have expired, hairline cracks or other hidden defects. In order to be sufficiently protected and still be able to breathe, a person should be fitted to a modern, tested gas mask designed for a particular use. For the average American, that's neither practical nor necessary.

THE COURAGE TO UNDERSTAND

Man's capacity for evil makes democracy necessary, and man's capacity for good makes democracy possible.

Reinhold Niebuhr

1. Why do you think someone would unleash a biological attack against an entire population of people?

_____

_____

_____

_____

2. Would you want your entire family to be vaccinated against potential biological threats, even if you knew it might cause a severe allergic reaction in a member of your family? Why or why not?

_____

_____

_____

_____

3. Should the government vaccinate all of us, no matter what the cost? What other government services would you be willing to give up (e.g., free education, free interstate highway systems) in order to offset the medical costs?

_____

_____

_____

_____

4. Is biological warfare more or less morally wrong than conventional warfare? Why or why not?

_____

_____

_____

_____

5. What should be done to countries or leaders who use biological warfare against others?

_____

_____

_____

_____

6. There are Americans who protest any military response we make to any attack on the United States. How do you feel about that?

_____

_____

_____

_____

DON'T JUST SIT THERE

I know not with what weapons World War III will be fought, but World War IV will be fought with sticks and stones.

Albert Einstein

1. Want to lower your risk significantly? Then listen to your mother and wash your hands often and well. Yes, that means with warm water and plenty of soap. It's still your best defense against germs.

2. Listen to what is going on around you and know the symptoms for any biological attack that might be suspected. Also learn to recognize how it is transmitted and what you can do about it.

3. Think about where, what and how you eat. Salad bars and buffets are just as convenient for germs as they are for you.

4. Have a family plan. Most schools require that your parents provide an emergency contact in case of illness or accident. Your family should also have an emergency plan. Ask your parents to sit down and talk about what each of you should do if there is a

credible biological threat. What other family members or close friends could you rely on in case of a medical emergency? What else should you know or do? Write the information down on index cards and have each family member carry a card at all times.

5. Know your doctor's phone number. Learn the phone number of your pharmacy. Find out your health insurance information and commit it to memory or write it down and keep it with you.

6. Make a conscious effort to stay healthy. Get sleep. Eat as well as you can. Exercise. A strong body is the best deterrent to disease.

7. Put together a family survival container. Include a stash of bottled water, ready-to-eat (sealed) food, a first-aid kit, flashlights, radio, plenty of batteries, extra eyeglasses, necessary medications and cash. If you have pets, make sure you include emergency provisions for them, as well. If necessary, during cold weather make up a second pack of winter gear, including warm clothing and blankets.

8. If you believe vaccines should be available to the general public for smallpox or other germ agents,

go online or ask your parent or social-studies teacher for a list of your Congressional representatives and write or call them with your concerns. Believe it or not, they listen, especially during times of crisis.

9. Dorothy was right: "There's no place like home." When it comes to disease, home is probably the safest place for you to be because most diseases are caught or transmitted outside the home. Don't stop going out, but be aware of the risks in crowded places.

10. Know your food sources and play it safe. Now may be the best time to learn to enjoy "home-grown" American foods. That may mean that you won't be eating raspberries in February or fresh cranberries in June, but we still have the greatest food variety of any country on Earth.

11. Remember that the CDC can provide you and your family with detailed information on these diseases. It exists for you and your protection. Use it. You can find the agency online at *www.cdc.gov* or call 800-311-3435.

WHAT ARE THE CHANCES?

Your level of threat can be assessed by determining the probability—or likelihood—of a particular risk factor affecting you, and the level of impact—or consequence—of that threat. Based on what you know about your lifestyle, your community, current threats you may face and what you have learned, rate the likelihood and the consequence of each of the following vulnerabilities. Then write the number of that vulnerability in the appropriate box on the matrix provided at the end of this chapter to assess your level of risk from the vulnerabilities listed. You are building a matrix that will include all the threats in this book.

VULNERABILITIES

5. Anthrax
6. Botulism
7. Smallpox
8. Plague
9. Rabbit fever
10. Mustard gas
11. VX

	CONSEQUENCES	
	LOW	HIGH
HIGH		
LOW		

LIKELIHOOD

Answers: How Much Do You Know?

1. d ▪ 2. b ▪ 3. d ▪ 4. d ▪ 5 .F ▪ 6. d ▪ 7. F ▪ 8. d ▪ 9. d ▪ 10. a

3

Dollars & Sense*

RISK SCENARIO—
WHAT WOULD YOU DO?

You didn't understand it until last night—why your mom and dad seemed so concerned about the nation's economy and family finances. You've seen that before: the year your mother quit her job and went back to school; the summer before your older sister started college; the September the flood wiped out your dad's accounting business. They were all family financial crises that were handled and, over time, diminished, although you did feel sometimes that the only real victim was you. While everyone else made adjustments, you made sacrifices. No car of your own, no holiday ski trip, no one-of-a-kind dress for prom. As a hedge against future disappointment, on your own, you sought and landed a part-time job working two nights a week and alternate Saturdays and Sundays as a clerk at an upscale store at the mall. You were building a little nest egg and still buying great clothes at a discount. You were enjoying greatly some measure of financial independence and had learned how to save a little money as the weeks rolled by. All was well. Until last night.

Well, actually, last night's crushing disappointment was a product of the September 11, 2001, attacks. And even though you had read and heard about the plummeting economy, you never thought it would touch you. Even when business slowed to a fraction of what it had been over the summer, you had no idea it would slow to the point of having Sara do what she did. Due to the sharp decline in business, you were laid off. Out of a job and with no back-up plan, you became a new victim of the terrorism that had touched so many lives.

Who would have thought that terrorists crashing planes into buildings in New York City and outside Washington, D.C., in Arlington, Virginia (yes, the

Pentagon really is in northern Virginia, not Washington, D.C., as many media reports would have you believe), would have affected you and your family in California months later? Why didn't someone prepare you for this? You didn't work for an airline or in the travel industry. Obviously, you didn't work for any of the companies that were destroyed, and neither did your parents. It doesn't seem fair that your life should be disrupted this way. You feel bad for the victims and their families. And you say a prayer every night for our soldiers and sailors overseas. But why should you be out of a job because of what terrorists did all the way on the East Coast?

You've heard your mom and dad say that their businesses—accounting for your dad, real estate for your mom—are suffering, too. People just aren't spending money like they used to do. It seems everyone is feeling the financial effect of what the terrorists did. But then you remember what your friend Kelley told you about the family that moved into her cul de sac last summer. They live in the biggest home in the neighborhood, the kids all wear nice clothes, the mother and oldest daughter just got new cars—expensive ones—and yet neither the mom or dad seem to work. They are always home during the day, and lots of people who, like them, appear to be from the Middle East, come and go while the kids are at school. The other day, when Kelley was with the younger daughter, the dad gave her a one-hundred-dollar bill to go to the mall on a shopping trip with Kelley. How could this be? With everyone else tightening their spending, what's going on with a family in which no one seems to work a regular job?

The more you think about it, the more it bugs you. And then you get annoyed that you are even thinking about it at all. Big deal—so they have money. Maybe they won the lottery or inherited it. Just because they appear to be Arabs doesn't mean they are terrorists or criminals. You feel bad about yourself for even thinking such a thing.

And yet, you recall a TV program warning people to look out for suspicious situations and activities. This was just the kind of thing they were talking about—people with no visible means of income spending lots of cash. It fits the profile. But you've heard your dad say how bad profiles are. Maybe you should discuss this with him. Then again, he is so busy, worried about his own money problems. And why should you stick your nose into other people's business just because they have plenty of money and you just lost your job?

Still, it's bugging you a lot. You hate it when you let things like this gnaw away at you. Maybe Mrs. Hansen, your economics teacher, would be a good person to talk with about this. What would be the harm in bringing it up tomorrow after class?

How Much Do You Know?

1. True or False: The nation's economy was already in trouble when the September 11, 2001, attacks happened.

2. The terrorist attacks will have what effect on the country's financial future?
    a. none
    b. the economy will be ruined by a financial depression
    c. the full impact is unknown, but it has already been negative
    d. they will help build up the economy

3. Who is most affected by downturns in the nation's economy?

    a. people in foreign countries

    b. the upper class in our country

    c. middle and lower income Americans

    d. bankers and investment advisors

4. In 2001, the cost of the war on terrorism was:

    a. 1% of our annual gross national product

    b. 10% of our annual gross national product

    c. 25% of our annual gross national product

    d. I don't know what the annual gross national product is, but I will look it up

5. Who bears responsibility for getting our economy running again?

    a. the president and Congress

    b. Alan Greenspan and the Federal Reserve

    c. bankers and investors

    d. every single one of us who cares about America

6. The best way for me to help with the war on terrorism and the nation's economic problems is to:

    a. spend every cent I have and can earn in a part-time job

b. work hard, save it all, spend nothing

c. let people who make real money worry about it

d. balance earning, saving and spending based upon what I've read and learned

7. My obligation to be aware of our economy and do what I can to help is:

a. zero; I'm a teenager with no job, a weak allowance and stingy parents

b. moderate; I'm a teenager, but I care and will be out on my own some day

c. significant; I worry about this all the time, as we all should

d. more than I can handle

8. My obligation to be aware of suspicious activities and situations in my community is:

a. zero; I am a teenager and shouldn't get involved

b. something I should take seriously

c. something I don't want to worry about

d. the same as every other responsible citizen's

Answers can be found at the end of this chapter.

MYTH VS. FACT

Expecting the Worst

Posterity! You will never know how much it cost the present generation to preserve your freedom! I hope you will make good use of it!

John Adams

The Myth: The only financial impact of terrorism is on the industry or site attacked. It will take years for other businesses and people to be affected, and by then the government will have our economy running strong again. Anyway, this is the government's responsibility, not mine. The real focus for terrorists is instilling fear by killing lots of Americans with bombs or viruses. They don't care about our money problems. They think we all are rich.

Understanding the Rest

We cannot direct the wind, but we can adjust the sails.

Anonymous

The Truth: Terrorists are out to disrupt this country by creating economic as well as emotional chaos. The attacks on September 11, 2001, were directed at two symbols of American strength and success: finance and the military. There have been many collateral and derivative effects of what the terrorists accomplished in New York City and just outside the nation's capital in Arlington, Virginia, with the crashes into the World Trade Center and the Pentagon, and the terrorists knew there would be. They intended those consequences. They hoped our faith in the government's ability to protect us would be shaken, if not destroyed. And they knew that business and financial activity well beyond that in the Twin Towers of the World Trade Center and surrounding buildings would suffer as a result of bringing those buildings down. They calculated an impact on the airline industry, tourism and commerce from a loss of confidence that flying is a safe way to travel. They knew that hotels, motels, restaurants and tourist attractions, and the businesses that support them, would suffer all over the country. They knew that people in Maine and Texas, Idaho and Florida, and all points in between would be affected. When another plane crashed, we would wonder if it was another attack before we would consider it an accident. Many would lose their jobs because people would stop traveling and spending money. Many people lost their lives in the attacks on September 11, 2001. For months, maybe years thereafter, many others will lose their livelihoods and be otherwise affected. We likely will not know the full impact of the terrorist attacks for many years.

IGNORANCE IS NOT BLISS

- Economists speak often of "trickle-down" effects of certain actions or conditions upon our economy. The trickle-down effect of terrorists' acts and the war on terrorism will touch us all in many ways.
- As people travel and spend less, some people will lose their jobs because their business has no customers to serve.
- The cost of doing business will go up for many companies. For example, packages containing goods will cost more to send and take more time to be delivered due to added security measures.

- Similarly, the cost of insurance for businesses will increase due to increased threats and risks.
- The cost of some goods and services will increase as business owners spend more to protect their employees and buildings.
- We all have responsibility for the financial well-being of our country. The nation's economy is a complicated structure that depends upon many factors for its health. Interest rates and investment, production and exporting, employment, and saving and spending are just some of the factors influencing our financial status.
- Your spending on clothes, sports, music, concerts, cosmetics, movies and food is a significant factor in determining the condition of the country's finances.
- Your ability to get a job now, and when you begin your career many years from now, will be affected by current economic conditions.

UNFAMILIAR, NOT UNCHARTED

1. Everyone talks about the cost of the war on terrorism, but what is the country really spending on response and recovery efforts as a result of the attacks?

The estimate for U.S. spending on terrorism-related issues in 2001 was more than $20 billion. That figure includes more than $7 billion for recovery and relief in New York City and at the Pentagon; $3 billion to fight bioterrorism; and nearly $3 billion for special security measures at airports, federal buildings, dams and power plants, and for aircraft.

2. How about for the military operations?

Another $20 billion in spending is the estimate for the war on terrorism in 2001.

3. That sounds like a tremendous amount of money. Can we afford this war?

Most leaders will tell you we cannot afford not to engage in this war. Our way of life is in jeopardy from terrorists who hate us and the manner in which we live. Although $40 billion is a great deal of money, it represents less than 1 percent of our annual gross national product, the value of all goods and services we produce each year. Most economic experts agree that to get our country's financial house back in order, the federal government is going to have to do even more to stimulate the economy.

4. Is fear a factor in dealing with economic conditions?

Of course. Uncertainty over our physical safety, as well as our financial security, causes investors and consumers to be more cautious, less active in the marketplace. This hurts business because fewer customers means reduced sales and profits. People get laid off from their jobs and have less money to spend. You can see why they describe it as a cycle.

5. I can understand why families have less money, but I thought the federal government and most states had budget surpluses. Why do we keep hearing about budget cuts?

There are two answers to that question. First, government budgets are built on projections of revenues, that is, how much money a government anticipates bringing in during a fiscal year. If the amount of money coming into government—through sales tax, income tax or other means—is reduced, the government has less to spend. Second, budgets often include significant increases in spending over previous years. So, sometimes a budget cut is a reduction in the amount of increase, not an actual reduction in the amount of current spending.

6. What is a fiscal year?

Governments typically do not operate on a calendar year, from January 1 through December 31. Instead, they set their spending year on a different schedule. For example, the federal government's fiscal year begins on October 1 and continues through September 30. Many state governments run on a July 1 to June 30 fiscal year.

7. How does a reduction in government spending affect me and my family?

It may mean a change in the services you receive. For example, some communities charge book rentals for textbooks, while in other communities that cost is covered in the community's budget. Some cities offer free recreation, but a cut in service might reduce the number of programs provided or the hours of operation, or it may mean that citizens will have to start paying fees for the programs.

8. On the one hand, we hear that we need to be careful to keep our personal debt low, and yet we hear government officials telling us to spend more money. How can we do both?

It's a balancing act. We need to spend money to keep the economy running, but no one should spend so much money that his own finances are in jeopardy. If you have significant savings, then you have a stronger safety net and you can probably afford to spend more than someone who has substantial debt. If you have debt, then spend money on necessities, but try to reduce your debt as quickly as you can.

9. Can war affect the economy in a positive way?

Definitely. When a country gears up to fight a war or to recover from a disaster, jobs often are created. And demand for certain items increases. Both of those factors are beneficial to an economy.

THE COURAGE TO UNDERSTAND

Our land is more valuable than your money. As long as the sun shines and the waters flow, this land will be here to give life to men and animals; therefore, we can not sell this land. It was put here for us by the Great Spirit and we can not sell it because it does not belong to us.

Blackfoot Chief (c. 1880)

1. What economic impacts of the terrorist attacks have you already seen?

_____

_____

_____

_____

2. How has any of that impact affected you directly?

_____

_____

_____

_____

3. Does your family have money in the stock market that was or may be affected by terrorist attacks?

_____

_____

_____

_____

4. What do your parents say about their strategies to protect their money and promote the nation's economy?

_____

_____

_____

5. What about your own money? What changes in your spending habits have you made since September 11, 2001?

_____

_____

_____

6. Do you think that severe attacks on our country could send the economy into another depression? Why or why not?

_____

_____

_____

_____

7. What are the "experts" saying about the economic future?

_____

_____

_____

_____

8. Why do you think terrorists target economic centers?

_____

_____

_____

_____

9. Do you think their tactic of demoralizing the country through economic means will be successful?

_____

_____

_____

_____

10. If you were the president, what one thing would you do to get our economy rolling and healthy again?

_____

_____

_____

_____

11. What one thing are you going to do right away to improve your financial picture?

_____

_____

_____

_____

DON'T JUST SIT THERE

Today you can go to a gas station and find the cash register open and the toilets locked. They must think toilet paper is worth more than money.

Joey Bishop

1. Talk to your parents about the current state of the economy and, if they are willing, about the family

financial picture. If your family needs to cut back, volunteer to be part of the solution, not the problem.

2. Be a contributor. Get a part-time job, if your schedule, grades and parents will permit it. You can help family finances by bearing the burden of some of your expenses.

3. Be a smart spender. Exercise more prudence about the things you spend money on. Our economy needs the fuel your spending provides, but you should not be frivolous. Buy what you need, but not always everything that you want.

4. Be a more responsible consumer. Take the time to learn more about money, finances, banking, investment and the economy. You are a player here. Teen spending is a huge market force. Producers of goods and services spend billions of dollars every year in efforts to attract your attention and obtain your business.

5. Be involved. Talk to your parents about the economic outlook for the country. Listen to what your teachers say and discuss these topics with them.

6. Think about ways economic downturns affect your school. If you normally hold your prom in an

upscale hotel, maybe you ought to suggest a change and use the gym instead.

7. Pay attention to the unemployment figures for your community. If growing numbers of workers lose their jobs, then growing numbers of families may need assistance. Can your school club help in any way?

8. Set an example. Instead of going out to dinner before the prom, why not eat at someone's house? You can still have a great meal by candlelight. After the prom, do the same; ask one of the parents to volunteer to cook breakfast for everybody.

9. Pay down your own debt, if you have any, including credit cards and money you owe to your parents.

10. If college is in your future, begin looking responsibly at the costs of the schools you are considering. Then get serious about looking at scholarships and grants.

WHAT ARE THE CHANCES?

Your level of threat can be assessed by determining the probability—or likelihood—of a particular risk factor affecting you and the level of impact—or consequence—of that threat. Based on what you know about your lifestyle, your community, current threats you may face and what you have learned, rate the likelihood and the consequence of each of the following vulnerabilities. Then write the number of that vulnerability in the appropriate box on the matrix provided at the end of this chapter to assess your level of risk from the vulnerabilities listed. You are building a matrix that will include all the threats in this book.

VULNERABILITIES

12. Loss of own job
13. Parent's loss of job
14. Loss of home
15. Loss of community services

	CONSEQUENCES	
	LOW	HIGH
HIGH		
LOW		

LIKELIHOOD

Answers: How Much Do You Know?

1. T • 2. c • 3. c • 4. a • 5. d • 6. d • 7. b • 8. b & d

4

Land of the Free*

It's been one of those days at school. You lost your English paper, although you're sure you stuffed it in your notebook. Who knows—maybe it fell out in the car. Then your math teacher threw a pop quiz at you. Because play practice ran so late last night, you didn't really have time to study. You thought you were safe; math quizzes usually pop up on Friday. To top it off, it's lunchtime and you can't find anyone. You have this sinking feeling that you are supposed to be meeting them somewhere else, maybe in the auditorium, but you can't remember.

77

Now Jaqui, who you barely know, wants to talk to you. Jaqui's family owns a small motel just off the interstate that's frequented by long-haul truck drivers and senior citizens. While the motel is clean and neat, it has seen better years.

As you walk toward the auditorium, Jaqui tells you that she's worried about four of the guests at the motel. They are foreign. They wear western clothing, but they keep to themselves. She has heard only one of them speak and his Arab accent was so thick she could hardly understand him. He told her he was a student at the community college, but she has never seen him with any books.

Jaqui's mother says that when she takes fresh towels and sheets to the rooms, they don't let her in. Instead, they thank her and take them at the door. Like Jaqui, she has only spoken to one of the men. They come and go at all hours of the day. They drive an old car with out-of-state plates. They buy food at a little grocery store about a mile from the motel. They always pay cash at the store, just like they do at the motel.

With everything that's gone on, Jaqui, her mother and her sisters are worried about these guests. What if they are terrorists? How would she know? Is Jaqui's family at risk of being harmed? Or are they just paranoid because there's been so much in the news about credible threats and terrorists living in this country? What is a credible threat anyway?

You near the auditorium and hear the laughter of your friends inside. Suddenly, it hits you how frightened Jaqui sounds in comparison. You stop for a minute as Jaqui asks your advice. Your family has lived here all your life, Jaqui tells you. You know everybody and everybody knows you.

What would you do if you were Jaqui? What do you tell her? How much do you know about foreigners visiting or living in this country? Could those men be terrorists? How many terrorists are there in America? Does Jaqui's story worry you?

How Much Do You Know?

1. How many people enter and exit the United States every year?

a. 10 million

c. 100 million

b. 50 million

d. 500 million

2. How many foreign students are living in the United States?

    a. 137,000   c. 565,000

    b. 298,000   d. 721,000

3. True or False: Visitors from Canada and Mexico do not need visas to visit this country.

4. True or False: Visitors from all other countries need visas to come into the United States.

5. Approximately how many visas does the United States issue in a year?

    a. 3 million   c. 10 million

    b. 7 million   d. 15 million

6. About how many Mexican workers are living illegally in the United States?

    a. 500,000   c. 3.5 million

    b. 2 million   d. 5 million

7. True or False: Imported food faces the same scrutiny by inspectors as food produced in this country.

8. Why is processed food generally considered to be safe?

    a. because it is heated

    b. because it is frozen

    c. because it is produced in the United States

    d. both a and b

9. How many people were killed in the 1995 sarin gas attack in Japan?

    a. 12   c. 1,200

    b. 120   d. 12,000

10. Approximately how many public water systems are there in the United States that could at least theoretically be contaminated by terrorists?

    a. 500   c. 15,000

    b. 1,500   d. 150,000

Answers can be found at the end of this chapter.

MYTH VS. FACT

Expecting the Worst

There are wars of choice, and there are wars of necessity. . . . A war of necessity is a life-or-death struggle in which the safety and security of the homeland are at stake.

Charles Krauthammer

The Myth: The terrorists have stolen our freedom. Increased security measures and heightened states of alert will take over our lives and drastically limit our liberties.

The terrorists may have killed thousands of Americans, but they have accomplished an even greater goal: They have shaken our free society. They have penetrated every system in our country, and no one is safe. Now our parents can't get into their places of work without ID cards. We can no longer travel freely as we once did. We can't send packages through the mail, and it's no longer safe to eat in ethnic restaurants. The government can't guarantee the safety of our water supplies or even the air we breathe.

Even more frightening, we don't know how many terrorists are still operating in this country. We don't know where they are living or where they will strike again. No community is safe.

Understanding the Rest

We are all soldiers now. We have been drafted by history. And we must be watchful and protective as soldiers. Second thing: It's good to think locally. Third thing: Carry a camera. Cameras may turn out to be the first and best twenty-first-century homeland defense weapon.

Peggy Noonan

The Truth: There is a vast difference between convenience and liberty. The "new normalcy," as Vice President Dick Cheney calls it, means we have lost some of our past conveniences. A change of lifestyle to be sure, but daily conveniences are not the same as our basic liberties.

Think for just a moment about an event that changed you. It may have been the death of a loved one or a car crash involving one of your friends. It may have been a stupid prank that went wrong. Or it may be something you said that you wish you could take back.

Before September 11, 2001, we Americans were living a pretty comfortable, actually cushy, life. We were so comfortable that we were fighting among ourselves, like children fighting over a toy. We talked a lot about our differences and very little about how much we share. It's amazing how an instant can change a single life or hundreds of millions of lives.

After the 1999 massacre at Colorado's Columbine High School, most schools changed their policies and procedures to increase students' safety. Some school districts required that students carry ID cards. In many communities, police officers began patrolling school buildings, parking lots and events. There was a significant crackdown on threats and potential weapons. Once in a while, a school or school district overreacted to a potential problem, but overall, safety was increased without infringing on the rights of students, staff or parents. You still have pep rallies and football games.

Cafeterias are still noisy, crowded places where you can go to complain about teachers and visit with your friends. Your hallways are still filled with laughter as you move between classes. Your freedoms remain intact.

In 1944, as his troops were facing battle during World War II, General George S. Patton said to them, "Don't be a fool and die for your country." Instead, he suggested, let the enemy die for his. Now the United States is facing a very different enemy, involved in another war that is being fought not just on foreign soil but on our own. An extremist terrorist finds glory in martyrdom. That is his choice. He can decide if he wants to sacrifice his life for his cause.

But that does not give him the right to take anyone in your school or your community or your nation with him. And while his twisted fanaticism finds glory in a radical martyrdom, our country was built on very different ideals—life, liberty and the pursuit of happiness. Our democracy was built on collective independence and individual freedom. Throughout our country's history, millions of soldiers have fought to protect those freedoms, and thousands are doing so today.

Meanwhile, you, your family and your friends can

continue to enjoy the liberties we cherish. You do not have to be given permission by our government to travel. You have the right (although you may not always think you want it) to a free public education. You can live where you choose, and your parents can work wherever they wish. None of our basic freedoms have been restricted. Is it so much to ask that we alter a few daily behaviors to help keep our schools and communities safe? It sounds far-fetched, but that is exactly what we are doing. And, even then, how much have we been asked to give up? We still take for granted the ability to walk into a room and turn on a light switch. We still expect to turn on a faucet and have clean water at our fingertips. Our roads are in good shape and other government services are still provided, without much thought on our part.

Many argue that America is standing taller today than it was before the attacks. Americans strongly support their government. We are kinder to one another. We are more patriotic than we have been since World War II. We are steadfast in our beliefs and calm in our actions.

So then the question is, what are the risks we face in our schools, neighborhoods, towns and cities? And what can we do about them? We don't know what the future will bring, but we do know what we had in the past and what we need to regain.

IGNORANCE IS NOT BLISS

- Whether you live to eat or eat to live, one thing is certain: Everybody needs food, which is why so many people are worried about our food supply. Fortunately, food processing in this country keeps many of our foods safe, often because they are heated through pasteurization, sterilization or cooking.

- Foods that are not processed—fresh meats, fruits and vegetables—pose more of a problem. If a disease like foot-and-mouth disease was introduced in this country, it could devastate large segments of our agricultural industry, just as it has in Great Britain. Authorities have stepped up agricultural research, looking for vaccines and other methods to reduce our vulnerability to bioterrorism.

- Imported food, on the other hand, poses a greater risk. Prior to the destruction of the World Trade Center, only about 1 percent of all the food imported into this country was inspected. Now, inspections have increased, as has security at American food-processing facilities.

- If food contamination is discovered, the federal government has a process in place to quickly recall it. In fact, the system is used fairly regularly to recall food that has been contaminated after packaging or when a contaminant is discovered at a food-processing center. Often, the system is used to recall meat products carrying a particular germ.

- Still, we have not been as vigilant as we now must be. In 1993, cryptosporidium, a disease usually found in feces, was discovered in the Milwaukee water system. Although the source of the contamination was never disclosed, hundreds of thousands of people were affected and officials estimate that more than fifty people died from the disease. The organism had survived treatment at the water plant, proving that we are vulnerable to attack through our water system.

- We are not, however, as vulnerable as we once were. There are more than 150,000 government water systems in the United States. Prior to the terrorist attacks of September 11, 2001, they were not well protected. In fact, most were readily accessible. Now, most communities are taking steps to secure those water supplies from attack. In many localities, access to water supplies via roads and waterways has been eliminated and sampling of the water supply has increased. In scores of large cities, federal, state or local law enforcement officers are helping to protect our water.

• Our water is further protected by the fact that most supplies are large enough to dilute many poisons even before treatment. Also, most water-treatment plants treat the water to remove harmful chemicals, further protecting customers from attack.

• Many communities offer mass transit systems including buses, metros and trains. The 1995 sarin gas attack on a Tokyo subway proved that such transit systems are at risk. Still, the risk may be less than you think. Aum Shinrikyo, the cult that perpetrated the Japanese nerve gas attack, had tried unsuccessfully, at least ten times, to launch a biological attack. While their chemical attack killed twelve people, that number was far less than the cult had hoped to murder.

- One challenge facing communities and the government is the issue of the "worried well." The anthrax outbreak showed us that many people become so fearful of catching a disease that they begin to exhibit whatever symptoms might reflect the disease. In other words, although they are not contaminated, they cause themselves to become ill by believing they have caught the disease. They threaten to overwhelm medical personnel, flooding doctors' offices, health clinics and emergency rooms seeking treatment. If a large-scale biological or chemical attack was to occur, the worried well could further stretch an already overworked health system.

- The anthrax outbreak also highlighted the vulnerabilities of our postal system. Every household in America has access to the post office, and our mail is often delivered directly to our front door. Now people worry, not just about contaminated mail, but also about cross-contamination. While the risk remains small, the government is taking steps to further insure our safety. In the meantime, everyone should wash his or her hands after handling the mail. More advice your mother would love.

• Do you know what your guaranteed rights are? How familiar are you with the Constitution of the United States of America? Some civil libertarians fear that the terrorist threat facing this country will limit our rights, if not by law, then by practice. Some college professors are finding that there is no longer a great public tolerance for those who fault U.S. foreign policy or are blatantly critical of government leaders. But public censure of anti-American speech is very different from legal actions that infringe on our rights. In extraordinary times, the key is to find the balance between protection of our civil liberties, both in law and in practice, and the ability to give government leaders the tools they need to protect our citizens.

UNFAMILIAR, NOT UNCHARTED

1. What is "anticipatory anxiety" and what can be done about it?

This is a type of psychological reaction that occurs when an individual can't recover from one event because he/she is so worried about what is coming next. So, if one terrorist event follows another, and then another follows that one, people can't work through the anxiety they feel. They remain afraid, unsure and anxious.

2. Most Americans have not been directly affected by a terrorist attack, so why are many people having trouble sleeping, concentrating and living normal lives?

One of the most basic human needs is the need to feel safe. Psychologists believe that if a person doesn't feel safe, then he/she won't be as likely to enjoy other parts of life like work, achievement and play. The fact that terrorists can reach American communities threatens the safety of all communities, not just those that have been directly affected by terrorist activities.

3. Why do adults keep telling kids to live their lives as normally as possible, even though, when we look around, we see that everything's changed?

Many people and communities were concerned about celebrating Halloween just weeks after the attacks on the World Trade Center and the Pentagon. But the chance that any one individual would be harmed by a terrorist on Halloween was very small. In the end, most parents chose to enjoy the fall tradition. Part of our responsibility in fighting terrorism is to help identify anything in the United States that might indicate a coming attack. Equally as important to the country, however, is our responsibility to promote the lifestyle and freedom of movement we cherish and continue to fight for.

4. What are the chances that other buildings will be attacked?

No one knows for sure. The likelihood of terrorists bombing homes or apartment buildings or small businesses is pretty slim; therefore, it should be one of the disasters that doesn't carry significant risk for most teens.

5. How safe are metros and other mass transit systems?

Again, no one can say for sure. City officials have stepped up security on most systems, just as they have for other government systems that can affect large numbers of people. With that said, if you regularly travel on a mass transit system, learn what to do in case of emergency. Do you know how to exit such a system? Do you know where emergency exits are? Do you know emergency procedures? Find out.

6. How likely is it that terrorists could attack one of our nuclear facilities?

Perhaps no other structures have been made more secure than our nuclear sites. They were built to withstand hurricanes, tornadoes and earthquakes. Altogether, there are 103 nuclear power plants in the United States. All of them are regulated by the Nuclear Regulatory Commission (NRC). Due to NRC oversight, the plants were built to exacting safety standards, and those standards have been upgraded and strictly adhered to. After the September 11, 2001, attacks, officials began to look at access security to the plants. Now, many are patrolled by state or federal forces. Even if one of them suffered a direct hit, a nuclear explosion would not result. Rather, the concern would be about the release of radioactive particles. For the most part, such an attack could be quickly handled because the power plants have strict evacuation and treatment plans in place and train on them regularly. Even in the 1979 Three Mile Island accident, no deaths occurred. Relatively speaking, the risk of a nuclear facility being breached is fairly low.

7. Could terrorists bring their own nuclear device in?

Theoretically, yes, and authorities aren't sure how to assess this risk. The United Nations, which tracks stolen radioactive materials, notes that there have been nearly four hundred illegal sales of such material since 1993. The greatest risk is probably a "dirty bomb," a conventional explosive "tipped" with nuclear material. Such a bomb could be set off in a community if terrorists have the materials to make such a device and the means to launch it. Experts know that terrorists are attempting to acquire nuclear weapons, and they do everything they can to track such attempts and prevent the acquisitions.

8. How long will it be until the United States is truly safe again?

The United States has never been able to fully guarantee your safety. Before you were born, your parents lived through several years of extraordinarily high crime rates. Many people were afraid to go out of their own homes, let alone travel freely. During your lifetime, traditional crime rates have been the lowest ever recorded in this country, but crime still occurs. Accidents still happen. No one can completely guarantee your safety. But, the government, over time, will continue to find ways to protect us from extremist terrorists who seek to destroy our way of life.

THE COURAGE TO UNDERSTAND

The human race has one really effective weapon, and that is laughter.

Mark Twain

1. What aspects of your everyday life make you feel the most secure and why?

_____

_____

_____

_____

2. What facets of your daily life make you feel the most vulnerable and why?

_____

_____

_____

_____

3. What specific steps can you take to increase your feeling of safety?

_____

_____

_____

_____

4. Are you more afraid in your school or community than you were before the September 11, 2001, terrorist attacks? Why or why not?

_____

_____

_____

_____

5. Does your family ever talk about current events and share feelings about what is going on? Is that a good thing for you or a bad thing?

_____

_____

_____

_____

6. Crises tend to make us think about our lives and how we are using them. Did the terrorist attacks on the World Trade Center and the Pentagon change the way you treat other people? In what ways?

_____

_____

_____

_____

7. Is there a deeper meaning to the terrorist activities that has caused your community to band together? If not, what would you suggest?

_____

_____

_____

_____

8. What would you do if you knew or saw someone who was acting suspiciously or whom you thought might be involved in an activity that could bring harm to your community?

_____

_____

_____

_____

DON'T JUST SIT THERE

Even if you're on the right track, you'll get run over if you just sit there.

Will Rogers

1. Set an example—for younger brothers or sisters, your friends and the adults around you. Remember, you can live your life by chance, or you can live your life by choice. Choose to make yours one of leadership and courage.

2. Just show up. Woody Allen once said that 90 percent of life is just showing up. It is also a way to fight terrorism. Terrorists want to change our daily

lives, so just "showing up" and "keeping on" helps win the battle against them.

3. Shop till you drop—within reason, of course. You bought stuff before this crisis, and now the country depends on our continuing to spend to keep the economy strong. Don't go overboard, but support our economy.

4. Learn as much as you can about the risks your community faces so that your opinions and understanding are based on knowledge, not just what you've heard. Read your local newspaper and listen to your local news every day.

5. Make it a habit to look for changes in your community that might raise concern. If you see anything or anyone that worries you, tell your parent, a teacher or another adult immediately.

6. Establish an emergency communication system for your family so that you can always reach each other, no matter what. And think about what you would do in the event of a national, state or local emergency if you were at school. Make sure you know your school's evacuation plan.

7. Know before you go. Many cities, counties, states,

public buildings and mass transit systems have changed the rules about what you can carry with you into public places and onto public transportation. Backpacks, coolers, totes and other similar items may be banned or searched. Parking rules have also changed in many places, including theme parks and ballparks.

8. Sometimes, when people feel extreme anxiety, they consume alcohol, smoke or engage in other problem behaviors. If your behavior changes, think about why. It is perfectly normal now for you to be experiencing additional stress, so talk to someone about it rather than engaging in dangerous behaviors.

9. Volunteer. Now, more than ever, this country needs volunteers. Do your part. Call your local hospital, fire station, or other public or private organization that needs help. If you don't know where to look, ask your parent or teacher.

10. Remember to keep life in perspective. It's amazing how so many of the problems we faced before September 11, 2001, now seem trivial. They probably are. Remember, as you worry about studying

for a test or think about what to wear on Friday night, that there are young adults—not much older than you—half a world away, fighting for our safety, our freedom and even our conveniences.

11. Be patriotic. Show how much you value your freedom. Stand when you hear our national anthem. Say the Pledge of Allegiance loudly. Wear a flag pin. Express, in as many visible ways as you can, that you support this country and all it stands for.

WHAT ARE THE CHANCES?

Your level of threat can be assessed by determining the probability—or likelihood—of a particular risk factor affecting you, and the level of impact—or consequence—of that threat. For example, your likelihood of being involved in a commercial jet crash is fairly low, but the consequences of such a crash are high. Conversely, your likelihood of being involved in a car crash during your lifetime is high, but the consequences are relatively low.

Based on what you know about your lifestyle, your community, current threats you may face and what you have learned, rate the likelihood and the consequence of each of the following vulnerabilities. Then write the number of that vulnerability in the appropriate box on the matrix provided at the end of this chapter to assess your level of risk from the vulnerabilities listed. You are building a matrix that will include all the threats in this book.

VULNERABILITIES

16. Food supply contamination
17. Water supply contamination
18. Postal contamination
19. Chemical/biological attack on mass transit system
20. Nuclear attack
21. Nuclear accident

CONSEQUENCES

	LOW	HIGH
HIGH		
LOW		

LIKELIHOOD

Answers: How Much Do You Know?

1. d ▪ 2. c ▪ 3. T ▪ 4. F ▪ 5. b ▪ 6. c ▪ 7. F ▪ 8. a ▪ 9. a ▪ 10. d

5

From Sea to Shining Sea

RISK SCENARIO— WHAT WOULD YOU DO?

Unbelievable. You knew it was going to happen, but now that it has, you can't believe it. First it was your ski trip and now your spring break plans for Cancun.

The ski trip was going to be incredible. You and close to a hundred of your classmates in the mountains for an extended weekend, surrounded by fields of snow, all the hot chocolate you could drink and all the hot skiers you could handle. You had plans to show up that arrogant jerk, Jason who thinks he's god of the slopes; you were gonna teach him better. You had plans to bunk with your

105

three best buddies. The four of you would have been raising hell—prank calls to your friends' rooms at three in the morning, raiding the minifridge and ordering pay-per-view. It would have been a perfect vacation.

Until the head honchos at the school freaked out and decided that traveling anywhere was "just too risky." After that one guy got thrown off a Greyhound bus for making threats, the administration doesn't want anyone traveling anywhere—especially out of state. Never mind the fact that you would've been on chartered buses, and you were only going a few hundred miles. So says the school board; so shall it be done.

Cancun was different. You didn't think anything could mess up your Cancun plans. Your parents had done the coolest thing ever—decided to take that trip over spring break and told you that you could bring two friends. Jamie and Becca were all for it, ready to go. You'd been saving your money so you could spend it all on sexy swimsuits and spa treatments. You had plans to spend some quality time with the sand and sun, soaking in the UV rays until you were golden brown. We won't tell your parents, but you also had secret plans to hook up with a hottie while you were down there, too. After all, mysterious strangers are made for romantic beaches. Even though the trip was months and months away, you had your bags mentally packed.

Too bad your parents decided it was—survey says: "Just too risky."

Now, this you really can't understand. Everything you're hearing says that planes are probably safer now than they've ever been. Sure, the extra security checks might be a hassle, but not enough to deter you from the beach. And it's not like you'd be headed even in the direction of any major city a terrorist might want to target.

Not to mention the fact that the trip wasn't until April. You're positive that things would have blown over by then. Everything would be back to normal, and planes would be just as safe as ever.

And now you have to disappoint your friends, too. You know they'll understand—Becca had plans to go to New York for Christmas that were canceled—but that's not the point.

It just doesn't seem fair that an event hundreds or thousands of miles away has to disrupt your life months in advance.

To put it simply, you're PO'd.

But at the same time, you're starting to get a little worried. There must be something to the school's claims if they'd go so far as to cancel the entire trip, right? And it's not like your parents to flip out for no good reason (unless you're a few minutes late for curfew, but that's another story).

You're also getting mixed messages from the media. Everyone's telling you to go back to your life, that the airlines are safer than ever, that we can't let the terrorists disrupt our lives. Simultaneously, they're telling you of breaches in security at national airports, warning you of credible threats and the need for "highest alert," and telling you that airport security must be increased even more. Any time anything happens to a commercial jet, the media questions whether the terrorists have struck again.

So, when being ticked wears off, you're just confused.

Who do you believe? Who's telling it like it is? Were your parents and the school administrators totally wrong for canceling your vacations? Or did they maybe have a point? And does this mean you're not going to get any vacations at all for a while? You think you'll go nuts if you have to stay in town until this is all over. So what can you do instead of taking faraway, extended vacations? Hey, there's a lake only a few hours' drive away—it's no Cancun, but it'll still have sun and water. Maybe you'll talk to your parents about that. And maybe you can get your friends together to convince the principal that while he might be right about canceling the ski trip, isn't there something else closer to home that he could organize?

What is happening to life as we knew it? Is all the fun soon going to be gone?

How Much Do You Know?

1. In the two months after the United States began its offensive against terrorism, there were how many incidents of terrorism at airports or involving air travel?

    a. a dozen   c. no one knows

    b. less than a dozen   d. none

2. Since the bombing raids in Afghanistan, air travel in this country has incurred:

a. minor delays, but little disruption
b. major disruption
c. there has been no air travel
d. no one knows

3. True or False: Travel in this country is important only to the tourism industry, and we can live without it.

4. True or False: Every year in this country millions of businessmen and -women travel millions of miles and conduct billions of dollars of business.

5. Travel, for reasons other than vacation, is:

a. unimportant
b. uninteresting
c. vital to the economic interests of the country
d. a perk that should be eliminated

6. Since 9-11, travel fares across the country are:
a. generally higher than ever
b. generally lower than ever
c. unchanged
d. nonexistent; I'm telling you, no one is going anywhere

7. Increased caution and security is important when traveling by:

a. plane

b. train

c. bus

d. car

e. cruise ship

f. all of the above, and every other conveyance

8. True or False: People aren't really afraid of flying or restricting their travel; that's just media hype.

9. True or False: Only commercial airliners, not private planes, pose a threat to safety as the result of a potential terrorist attack.

10. Travel in our country will:

a. go back to normal on October 5, 2003

b. go back to normal after we win the war against terrorism and terrorists

c. never be the same, but will be manageable with some adjustments

d. stop

Answers can be found at the end of this chapter.

MYTH VS. FACT

Expecting the Worst

I'm an idealist: I don't know where I am going but I'm on my way.

Carl Sandburg

The Myth: The safety of mass travel systems and conveyances can never be assured; therefore, you shouldn't fly, take a train, or ride a bus or metro. And because that means there will be way too many people driving on our highways, you should stay off them also. Travel, as we knew it, is over. We are approaching a time, very soon, when you will be able to travel only in the event of an emergency. Government has no plan and our people no will for dealing with what some dismiss as a matter of mere inconvenience, but what in truth is the end of the mass movement of people in our country.

Understanding the Rest

To travel hopefully is a better thing than to arrive.

Robert Louis Stevenson

The Truth: We cannot go back to the total conven- ience we once enjoyed in our mass transit systems, but there is much that is being done to ensure our safety. The truth of the matter is that all methods of travel we employ require extra care and caution to be safe.

Travel is not just something we do for fun or to reach a vacation destination; it is a vital component of the commerce of our nation and the world. Even with tech- nology and the Internet, everyday business requires the movement of people and the shipment of goods and services. These are not matters of convenience, but constitute necessities of life. From the clearly critical, such as the relay of donated organs for transplanta- tion to the routine shipment and delivery of mail and packages, our pursuit of life, liberty and happiness depends upon travel.

This is not to say that we have a constitutional right to travel as we wish, free of regulation and restriction. To accommodate the "new reality" since 9-11, we will have to endure some adjustments and inconvenience for the sake of making travel as safe as possible. Our safety and that of millions of others who travel the highways, airways, railways and waterways of the planet will depend upon all of us being a little more cooperative and a lot more tolerant than we have had to be in this country before September 11, 2001.

IGNORANCE IS NOT BLISS

Standing in the middle of the road is very dangerous; you get knocked down by the traffic from both sides.

Margaret Thatcher

- Care, caution and added security are necessary to make travel in our country as safe as possible.
- No amount of care, caution or added security will guarantee your safety—anywhere—traveling or sitting on the couch in your family room.
- There aren't enough police officers and National Guard troops in the country to completely guard every commercial airport, train and bus station, bridge, tunnel, dam and highway in the country.
- If we hired and trained one hundred new police officers and one hundred new National Guard troops every week for a year, we still would not have enough security to completely guard every commercial airport,

train and bus station, bridge, tunnel, dam and highway in the country.

- Even if we could completely guard every commercial airport, train and bus station, bridge, tunnel,
dam and highway in the country twenty-four hours a
day, safety could not be guaranteed.

- Don't forget the mail! Every day, millions of pieces of
mail move across this country by plane, train and
truck. A delay in travel means a delay in mail delivery.

- There are more than 220,000 private planes in this
country.

- Most private planes fly out of the nation's 4,700 small,
"general aviation" (noncommercial) airports, which
are not subject to federal security requirements.

- Most private planes have locks easier to pick than
the one on your locker at school.

- About 90 percent of the private planes in the nation
are registered in the name of corporations or lending
institutions, making it nearly impossible to trace the
people who own them.

- There are more commercial airline flights in
America per day than many countries, such as Israel,
have in a year.

UNFAMILIAR, NOT UNCHARTED

If all the cars in the United States were placed end-to-end, it would probably be Labor Day weekend.

Doug Larson

1. Are there any forms of travel not impacted by the terrorists' attacks and the war on terrorism?

No. All forms of travel, indeed, all aspects of the way we conduct our lives, have been influenced to some degree. Not all of this is a bad thing. While travel may take longer and inconvenience may increase, most of us are thinking more about safety and awareness. A lot of us are doing more to look out for others around us and create a safer environment to live life to its fullest.

2. Does the "new reality" of dealing with terrorism threats mean that more of us may be forced to travel alone in our own cars?

Ironically, no. In the short term, that has been the effect. More people are driving longer distances to avoid the perceived threat to travel by air or rail. But as highways become more congested as a result, safety there will be adversely impacted (more vehicles means a greater chance of being involved in a crash), and people will look back to mass transit as a way to move from place to place. Travel by plane and train remains very safe compared to all other forms, and added security measures will make them even safer.

3. What concerns people the most about flying and other forms of travel?

Fear of the unknown bothers most of the people who have any concern. The unknown for today's traveler isn't necessarily fear of another terrorist attack. Fear of undue delay, inconvenience, missing connections, and having business and personal interests adversely affected are top concerns.

4. Is the government really concerned about any of this, or is it all media hype?

The government, your political leaders, and thousands of federal, state and local public safety, health and transportation officials, are very concerned and are working diligently to solve problems, keep you safe, and infringe on your freedom and mobility as little as possible.

THE COURAGE TO UNDERSTAND

A person travels the world over in search of what he needs and returns home to find it.

George Moore

1. How has your family usually traveled in the past? Why did you choose to travel this way?

_____

_____

_____

_____

2. Are you afraid to travel now? Why or why not?

_____

_____

_____

_____

3. What's the furthest you've ever been from home? Would you travel there again now?

_____

_____

_____

_____

4. Would you feel safer traveling inside the United States or to a foreign country now? Why this choice?

_____

_____

_____

_____

5. Have you cut back on your travel in the past few months, or will you for upcoming vacations or holidays?

_____

_____

_____

_____

6. Have you changed your typical method of traveling? In what ways?

_____

_____

_____

_____

7. Would you feel safest in a train, plane, bus or car? Why?

_____

_____

_____

_____
_____

8. Did you or members of your family travel during the Gulf War in 1991? Did you have the same concerns then as you do now?

_____
_____
_____
_____

9. What do you think travel will be like in a year? Five years?

_____
_____
_____
_____

10. Where were you when the planes crashed on September 11, 2001?

_____
_____
_____
_____

DON'T JUST SIT THERE

Everywhere is walking distance if you have the time.

Steven Wright

1. Be proactive. Plan your trips—large and small—and allow plenty of time to reach your destination safely.
2. Be informed. Keep up-to-date through the media and industry about changes in travel standards, requirements, schedules, rates, fares and conditions.
3. Be helpful. Lend a hand to others through information you have or the physical abilities you possess to make their travel more pleasant.
4. Be alert. Whether you are driving the family car or your own if you are so fortunate, or traveling on a public conveyance, be aware of what is going on around you. Report suspicious or threatening activities or situations to appropriate authorities.
5. Be careful. Safety begins with you. Take special care and be cautious in all you do as you move about.

6. Be prepared. Help your family establish a family disaster plan, including a family escape route with meeting places both close to and some distance from home, and prepare personal "go bags" containing a change of clothes, foul weather gear, personal items and toiletries and enough food and water to sustain you for at least three days.

7. Be a leader. Set a good example for safety, security and citizenship, and be sure to follow your own standards. You can do more than you may realize to influence the attitudes and behaviors of those around you. In these challenging times, one right move can save a life—and the life you save may be your own.

WHAT ARE THE CHANCES?

Your level of threat can be assessed by determining the probability—or likelihood—of a particular risk factor affecting you and the level of impact—or consequence—of that threat. Based on what you know about your lifestyle, your community, current threats you may face and what you have learned, rate the likelihood and the consequence of each of the following vulnerabilities. Then write the number of that vulnerability in the appropriate box on the matrix provided at the end of this chapter to assess your level of risk from the vulnerabilities listed. You are building a matrix that will include all the threats in this book.

VULNERABILITIES

22. Being in a plane crash
23. Being in a hijacked train
24. Being in a metro/bus station when terrorist event occurs
25. Being on a metro or bus taken over by terrorists

CONSEQUENCES

	LOW	HIGH
HIGH		
LOW		

LIKELIHOOD

Answers: How Much Do You Know?

1. d ▪ 2. a ▪ 3. F ▪ 4. T ▪ 5. c ▪ 6. b ▪ 7. f ▪ 8. F ▪ 9. F ▪ 10. c

6

Instant Mess(age)

RISK SCENARIO— WHAT WOULD YOU DO?

You find yourself daydreaming in school. For the first time in days, the sun has won out over the clouds, and you want to be outside. It's only March, but you feel as if you've been in the same classes forever, and they're all boring. You've got spring fever, and you've got it bad. You need a break, if not physically, then mentally.

That night, as you chat with your friends and surf the Net, someone sends you an e-mail entitled "Beach Party, Open Me Now!" Wow, as if in answer to your daydreams, someone has sent you a virtual beach party.

You don't recognize the name of the sender and you know your parents will kill you if you open anything that causes problems with your computer, but you'd really like to jump into that beach party. So you do, just for a minute, but that's all it takes. Up pops a nasty-gram informing you that you've just infected your hard drive with a virus that will eat into all your files.

Pounding the mouse on the desk, you shut the file and delete it, hoping it was just a harmless prank. You can forget going out this weekend, or any weekend in the near future for that matter, if you've screwed up the computer!

You continue your IM conversations with your friends, and every once in a while you visit a chat room. All the time, that anonymous e-mail nags at you. Is a virus gnawing through your files at that very moment? Who sends that stuff, anyway? Why do people get their jollies by messing with other people's stuff?

Suddenly, your screen goes black. Then the image of a large garbage truck appears at the edge of your monitor. As it travels across your darkened screen, it spews out little floppy disks. When it disappears at the other end of the monitor, your computer shuts down.

Now what? You count to fifteen (well, really to six) and turn it on again. Nothing. You repeat the process, this time waiting the full fifteen seconds. Still no luck. Tiny beads of sweat appear on your forehead. You are concentrating so hard that you jump when the phone rings. It's Colin, one of your closest buddies.

"I just had the strangest thing happen to my PC," he tells you. "You're not gonna believe this thing that just got into my sys—"

"Was it a garbage truck?" you ask before he can finish.

"How'd you know? Hey, hang on. Somebody's beepin' in." The phone clicks and his voice disappears. Within a minute, he's back on. "It just happened to Matt-man, too. He said they're talking about it on the news. The word's not good, buddy. Apparently this thing is huge."

Now's your moment of truth. You try your computer one more time. Nothing. Time to let your parents know and deal with the consequences. Or you could just leave the computer off and pretend like everything's okay. Then whoever uses it next will take the fall.

Yeah, maybe that's the way to do it. The people who create those viruses ought to have to come live with your father for a week or two. That would cure them, you think as you get up and head out of the family room. Never once does it cross your mind that what you've just experienced is a weapon of mass disruption that has spread to millions of computers across the country. Within hours, hundreds of thousands of Americans will no longer have access to the Internet, chat rooms or Instant Messaging. And that's just the beginning. . . .

How Much Do You Know?

1. MAE East is the name of:

 a. an actress

 b. an Internet traffic exchange

 c. the government's secret cyber security site

 d. the first known computer virus

2. Which of the following federal agencies received a failing grade for cyber security?

 a. Department of Agriculture

 b. Department of Justice

 c. Department of Defense

d. all of the above

e. a and c

3. True or False: Our water supplies are generally safe from cyber attack.

4. How did the Code Red virus infect computer systems?

    a. by scanning the Web for vulnerable sites

    b. through e-mail distributions

    c. it was spread through Internet service providers

    d. no one knows yet how it spread

5. Why is it so easy to commit cyber-crime?

    a. because it's impossible to trace true hackers

    b. because the Internet structure is so full of holes

    c. because there are no strict laws against it

    d. because it is so profitable

6. What is Carnivore?

    a. a virus from South America

b. the code name for a famous terrorist

c. a cyber-surveillance program

d. the cyber-crime team at the FBI

7. True or False: Computer networks are prime terrorist targets.

8. How many American homes use the Internet for communication?

a. 60,000   c. 6,000,000

b. 600,000   d. 60,000,000

9. How many households worldwide are on the Net?

a. 4.25 million   c. 425 million

b. 42.5 million   d. no one knows

10. The Nimda virus, which appeared following the September 11, 2001, attacks, affected more than:

a. 50,000 computers

b. 500,000 computers

c. 1 million computers

d. 10 million computers

Answers can be found at the end of this chapter.

MYTH VS. FACT

Expecting the Worst

It's incredibly positive for the Internet.

> Raymond Oglethrope, president of AOL, discussing the
> impact of the anthrax attacks on the U.S. Postal Service

The Myth: Our nation has become completely dependent on the Internet. A terrorist hacker could not only shut down the entire internet system, but also could shut down our entire country.

A widespread Internet attack could interrupt communications across the country, making it impossible for us to communicate with one another, use electricity, fly our planes or move our money supply. Such an attack is possible because there are several physical locations where the Internet system could be attacked. Or cyber-terrorists could find a way to use the Internet to shut itself down, either by starting a new virus or by breaking into our key systems.

Such an attack, if successful, would then allow terrorists to follow up with a more conventional attack on the country. An attack that brings down the Internet could be the first shot in the final battle.

Understanding the Rest

Whatever needs to be maintained by force is doomed.

Henry Miller

The Truth: Any thought that an attack on one sector of the American infrastructure would be positive for another sector is misguided. The Internet, like the U.S. Postal Service, the airline industry and our road system, is an integral part of the framework that enables our country to run smoothly. An attack on one segment of our infrastructure quickly spills over into others. So the first realization is that Americans need to protect all the systems that provide the scaffold for our society, including our communications systems.

But can we? Have we become so dependent on the Internet that we have stopped creating back-up systems should it fail? When it does crash, how long does it take to get it up and running again? Could a terrorist organization use the Internet or some type of mobile communication system to attack us? Could a cyber attack be the first type of attack, followed by a more conventional, more deadly scenario?

Fortunately, this country had a dress rehearsal with Y2K. Because governments anticipated that computer systems might fail on January 1, 2000, billions of dollars were spent creating back-up capabilities. Our communications systems now have many redundancies and securities built in. While they are still vulnerable to attack, they are not as susceptible as they once were.

The Internet is a good example. First, it does not rely on a centralized system. In the past, there were physical locations in the country through which most Internet traffic passed. But procedures were changed and the function decentralized. If one area or site is attacked today, other areas can be used to reroute traffic.

IGNORANCE IS NOT BLISS

- The United States is becoming increasingly dependent on electronic communications, especially the Web. E-government and e-business allow people to communicate more rapidly, conduct business and use services. Unfortunately, it also leaves the nation open to cyber attack, sometimes known as the "weapon of mass disruption."

- On July 19, 2001, the Code Red worm raised its ugly head, scanning the Internet and finding vulnerable systems. It then installed itself into them and infected more than a quarter of a million computer systems in just nine hours. The threat was so real that Microsoft, the U.S. National Infrastructure Protection Center and the Federal Computer Incident Response Center all responded to the situation.

- The Code Red worm was quickly followed by the Nimda (some suggest the name refers to "Admin" spelled backwards) virus, which shut down many business and government operating systems. Like the Code Red virus, Nimda worked by scanning the Web, searching for and attaching to vulnerable systems. Even when Nimda was identified and thwarted, it disrupted access to the Internet for many users and, in some cases, took entire sites offline. In communities that lost computer capabilities, residents couldn't access public records, pay taxes or communicate with government officials.

• An especially unsettling fact is that the federal government's Web sites are not particularly secure. In September 2000, most government agencies (including the Departments of Defense, Commerce, Energy, Justice and Treasury) received a D grade on their computer security report card developed by the General Accounting Office (GAO) for Congressional investigators. A year later, instead of improving, most had dropped to an F grade. Many of these agencies maintain files with sensitive information that is vital to communities, states and even national security.

• According to the GAO, the systems of two dozen agencies are full of weaknesses and security lapses. The IRS, for example, according to the report, is vulnerable to hackers who can gain access to private taxpayer information.

• Our 911 emergency system is also at risk. Cyber-terrorists can devise programs that flood a system with so many calls that the system crashes. When that happens, legitimate emergency calls cannot get through to dispatchers.

- Business, too, is increasingly reliant on the Web. Our banking system is particularly vulnerable to cyber attack. Electronic money transfer is not new. In fact, it is nearly a century old. The Federal Reserve, the system that manages our money supply, began transferring funds through a private telegraph system in 1918.

- Today, there are three primary systems that support the electronic transfer of funds. These networks, run by the government and the banking industry, pass through ten processing centers. These centers, whose locations are kept secret, are vital to our nation's economy. If all ten were destroyed at once, it could create a significant fiscal crisis.

- Another vital function, air traffic control, also is increasingly dependent on computer systems. If the air traffic control network were attacked, it would put thousands of airline passengers at immediate risk.

UNFAMILIAR, NOT UNCHARTED

1. How often are cyber-terrorists trying to break into major systems in order to bring down the Internet?

There are potential attacks on Internet sites almost constantly—literally tens of thousands every year. Not all of them are cyber-terrorists. Some are just kids who are bored or who want to hack in just to see if it can be done. Because firewalls and other protective measures are constantly being upgraded, the likelihood of a catastrophic failure is relatively small.

2. How great is the risk that hackers can infiltrate personal computers in our nation's homes?

There is always the risk that any computer connected to the Internet can be accessed by a hacker or a cracker. It is, however, unlikely that terrorists would be interested in gaining control of your home PC. Far greater damage could be caused by shutting down government or business systems.

3. Is it true that past viruses have crippled the communications systems for entire cities?

There have been viruses, including Nimda, that disrupted computer systems for communities, disabling most government offices from working online. Yet even in those cases, the government remained open, even though the computer system was down. The critical element is the amount of time it takes to get back online.

4. What is the difference between a hacker and a cracker?

A hacker is considered someone who breaks into a site just to see if it can be done. Often, it plays out like a game for the hacker. He takes personal pleasure in infiltrating a site. A cracker, on the other hand, hacks into a system with the intent to conduct criminal activity such as identity theft. So a cracker is a CRiminal hACKER.

5. What is the difference between a cracker and a cyber-terrorist?

A cracker is often a lone individual or isolated group that is cracking into Web sites for financial gain. Cyber-terrorists, on the other hand, share the same goal as more traditional terrorists, that is, to wreak havoc and cause widespread chaos. Cyber-terrorists seek to destroy our systems in order to destroy our way of life and our faith in our government.

6. Are the criminal penalties for cyber-terrorism as tough as the penalties for traditional terrorists?

After the terrorist attack on September 11, 2001, Congress passed and the president signed a bill creating stiff penalties for cyber-terrorism. The U.S. Patriot Act, as it is called, enables the FBI to surveil and track Internet users. The agency no longer needs a court order to do so.

7. What is the Moonlight Maze?

Moonlight Maze is an ongoing attack on U.S. Web sites that was first discovered in March 1998. Since that time, federal investigators have been tracking its movements. Although we aren't sure how many of our systems it has successfully hacked into, we do know that it has stolen top secret files from the Pentagon and the National Aeronautics and Space Administration (NASA).

8. Has anyone ever broken into the power grid system in the United States?

In 1997, the federal government put together a team of thirty-five hackers to conduct a test of our nation's computer defenses. During the project, known as "Eligible Receiver," the team posed as foreign cyber-terrorists, and they were successful in breaking into power grids in nine cities. Another test, called "Zenith Star," was conducted in 1999 with similar results.

9. How significant is the threat of a terrorist actually destroying the Internet by targeting the physical locations of Internet providers?

Such an attack still would not shut down the Internet. The system is so decentralized, with routing hubs throughout the United States, that one or two strikes would not accomplish the goal of destroying the Internet.

10. What can be done to improve the security of our cyber systems?

In the wake of September 11, 2001, the government has redoubled its efforts to enhance the security of our most vital computer networks. The federal government is also looking at building its own secure intranet, called Govnet. In the long term, we need to train more cyber- security specialists. If you are looking for a career with great pay, interesting work and job security, consider cyber security. It's vital to our country's future.

THE COURAGE TO UNDERSTAND

Be willing to be uncomfortable. Be comfortable being uncomfortable. It may get tough, but it's a small price to pay for living a dream.

Peter McWilliams

1. How dependent are you on your computer? If you lost it, would your world change significantly?

_____

_____

_____

_____

2. When was the last time you opened an e-mail from someone you didn't know? Do you think it put you at risk?

_____

_____

_____

_____

3. Have you ever received a threatening or explicit e-mail? What did you do about it?

_____

_____

_____

_____

4. In light of the risk of a large-scale cyber attack, if you received a threatening e-mail tomorrow, what would you do?

_____

_____

_____

_____

5. Is there anyone in your house who knows more about computers than you? Given how much you know, what steps can you take right now to increase your family's cyber-security?

_____

_____

6. How would you feel if you knew someone had accessed your e-mail? How stiff should the penalties be for such an act?

DON'T JUST SIT THERE

Those who expect to reap the blessings of freedom must undergo the fatigue of supporting it.

Thomas Paine

1. Make sure you have up-to-date antivirus software loaded on your personal computer and use it.
2. Don't open e-mails from individuals whose names you don't recognize.
3. Ask your social studies or history teacher if your city or county government is reliant on e-government,

then find out if officials have back-up or contingency plans.

4. Find out if your family's utilities rely on the
Internet for vital services. Although they often use
layers of protection, they are not fail-safe. If, for
example, your power company's power grids are
controlled via computers, make sure your family
has an alternate plan should you lose power—
especially in the winter.

5. If your family relies on Internet communications,
make sure you have a back-up plan, especially in
case of an emergency.

6. Find out if your medical records are only kept
electronically. If they are, ask your parents to
request and keep up-to-date paper copies in case
you need them during a large-scale cyber attack.

7. If you have a savings account or a checking
account, find out how your bank keeps records. If
it relies on electronic bookkeeping, make sure
you keep your own accurate records of your
transactions (preferably in paper copy).

8. Check to see what your Internet service provider (ISP)
offers in the way of virus protection. Then use it.

9. Consider keeping a cache of family cash on hand, in case your family's bank experiences an electronic attack.

10. Stay in touch with what's going on in cyber-security. If you hear about a cyber attack that might affect you, find out as much as you can to protect yourself.

WHAT ARE THE CHANCES?

Your level of threat can be assessed by determining the probability—or likelihood—of a particular risk factor affecting you and the level of impact—or consequence—of that threat. Based on what you know about your lifestyle, your community, current threats you may face and what you have learned, rate the likelihood and the consequence of each of the following vulnerabilities. Then write the number of that vulnerability in the appropriate box on the matrix provided at the end of this chapter to assess your level of risk from the vulnerabilities listed. You are building a matrix that will include all the threats in this book.

VULNERABILITIES

26. Attack on home computer
27. Loss of utilities for a sustained period of time
28. Loss of electronic communications for a sustained period of time
29. Loss of emergency 911 because of cyber attack
30. Collapse of the Internet
31. Collapse of American financial system due to a cyber attack

	CONSEQUENCES	
	LOW	HIGH
HIGH		
LOW		

LIKELIHOOD

Answers: How Much Do You Know?

1. b ▪ 2. d ▪ 3. F ▪ 4. a ▪ 5. b ▪ 6. c ▪ 7. T ▪ 8. d ▪ 9. d ▪ 10. c

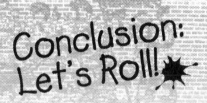

Conclusion:
Let's Roll!

If it is to be, it is up to me.

"Best Ten Two-Letter Words"
Source Unknown

What we've tried to do in this book is to provide you with information so that you can accurately assess your own level of risk for most of the challenges facing this country and the American people. It is not enough to know what threats are out there. It is more important to understand them and still more crucial to be able to evaluate how they impact you.

At the end of each chapter, you completed a matrix assessing the hazards presented as they relate to you and your situation. Now it's time to compile all that information into a single matrix. Take the results from the six chapters and transfer them to the summary matrix on the next page.

This will give you your own "big picture" of the current situation. We suggest you complete this final matrix in pencil because, as events occur and your environment changes, your risk factors will change accordingly. Hopefully, most of your vulnerabilities will fall into the "low likelihood, low risk" cell of the matrix. Pay more attention to those that fall within the "high likelihood" cells. Do whatever you can to reduce your vulnerability.

Teens (and adults) have asked us if this matrix can be used to address other parts of their lives. The answer, of course, is yes. It is not our matrix. In fact, it is the same one that is used by terrorism specialists to assess threats to communities, states and countries. It's a great decision-making tool, and we hope you use it in as many ways as possible. Mostly, we hope it helps you and those you love to stay safe.

We will not waiver; we will not tire; we will not falter; and, we will not fail.

President George W. Bush

		CONSEQUENCES	
		LOW	HIGH
LIKELIHOOD	HIGH		
	LOW		

Postscript: The Sleeping Giant

I fear all we have done is to awaken a sleeping giant and fill him with a terrible resolve.

Admiral Isoroku Yamamoto, as portrayed
in the 1970 film, Tora! Tora! Tora!

You are already being called the 9-11 generation, defined by a moment in time, not of your choosing, by an enemy you probably didn't know you had. How many times have you sung our national anthem, mouthing the words in rote memory, "Land of the free and the home of the brave"? But now you understand the true meaning behind those words. And your destiny. As much as your parents wish this war had never been visited upon you, visited upon any of us, it has, and your generation will continue to be tempered by it. Perhaps your life will even be divided by it. Perhaps you will talk of the days "before the World Trade Center" with the wistfulness of a child. Or perhaps you will come to believe that the events of September 11, 2001—the worst of times— brought out the best in us. And that, as horrific as it was, we are a far better people for it. A united family.

During World War II, after the Germans had overtaken many parts of Europe, and when the British were endur- ing nightly bombing raids by the Germans, they learned to go on with their daily lives. Even though thousands were killed, Winston Churchill, the prime minister of Britain, stood firm and determined, and his people stood with him. "We shall not flag or fail," he declared in 1940. "We shall go on to the end. . . . We shall fight on the beaches, we shall fight on the landing grounds, we shall fight in the fields and in the streets, we shall fight in the hills; we shall never surrender." And stand firm they did. And they, with the United States and our allies, were victorious.

There's a line from an old song, "You don't know what you've got 'til it's gone." You may have lost your innocence on that tranquil September morning. We assuredly lost the belief that we are invincible. But through the awesome terror of that day, we gained a unity and a resolve no one can defeat.

Hopefully now you have a clearer understanding of the threats facing our country and how they may impact you. We are armed with determination, knowledge and conviction. You will not be paralyzed by unknown threats. You will not let the terrorists win. You will not allow them to arbitrarily change your life.

You have plenty of places to look for heroes. They include the firefighters, police officers, medics and other first responders who rushed in on September 11, 2001, to save others, not thinking about their own safety. They are the men and women of United Flight 93 who attacked the hijackers and likely saved countless more lives. They are your grandparents and great-grandparents who fought to keep us free. They did what they did for your parents and for you. You are American. You are independent. You are free.

You always have been, of course, but perhaps never as free as you are today, because now you know just how precious our freedom is. Hold tight to it, fight for it, and spread it wherever and whenever you can. It is a priceless right.

Donna K. Wells and Bruce C. Morris

About the Authors

Donna K. Wells is the Assistant Secretary of Public Safety for the Commonwealth of Virginia responsible for policy, planning and program development, as well as coordination and funding for domestic preparedness activities. She also directed *4 SAFE VA,* the governor's school safety initiatives, and served as the Executive Director of the governor's New Partnership Commission for Community Safety. She speaks regularly at national conferences and workshops on youth safety and criminal-justice planning issues. Wells also serves as a faculty member of Virginia Commonwealth University's Commonwealth Educational Policy Institute and is a member of the Congressional Safety and Security Council.

Prior to assuming her current position, Wells served as the Policy and Planning Coordinator for the Virginia Department of Criminal Justice Services (DCJS). In that capacity, she served as liaison to the Criminal Justice Services Board and the U.S. Department of Justice. Wells also served as the state Youth and School Safety Specialist and developed numerous school and youth safety programs and initiatives. She was also instrumental in the development of the national Serious Habitual Offender Program. Wells began her career as a high-school English and reading specialist.

Wells has also authored or coauthored articles in numerous publications and journals, including *Police Chief, The Journal of Juvenile and Family Court Judges, The National School Safety Journal, The Journal of Police Science and Administration* and *Law and Order.* For several years, she wrote a weekly newspaper column, *It's Elementary,* for the (Norfolk, Virginia) *Virginian-Pilot and Ledger-Star.* The column was syndicated to several other newspapers. Additionally, Wells has published five nonfiction children's resource books.

In addition to her research and writing, Wells's professional affiliations have included the Virginia

Preparedness and Security Panel on Terrorism, the Virginia Department of Education School Violence Task Force, the Southeast Regional Center for Drug-Free Schools and Communities, Class Action, the Youth Alcohol and Drug-Abuse Prevention Project, the Virginia Partnership for the Prevention of Youth Violence, and the Virginia Association of Law Enforcement Explorer Advisors.

Bruce C. Morris serves as Chief Deputy Secretary of Public Safety for the Commonwealth of Virginia. In addition to the daily operational oversight of eleven public-safety agencies, Morris supervises the state's domestic preparedness initiatives, serving as the governor's coordinator for terrorism preparedness and as chairman of the state domestic preparedness multi-agency working group. He is the Coordinator for the Virginia Preparedness and Security Panel on Terrorism and a member of the Congressional Safety and Security Council. By designation of the governor, he is the FBI Single Point of Contact for the Commonwealth on Weapons of Mass Destruction issues and programs, and the Single Point of Contact to the national Homeland Security Office. Additionally, he, with coauthor Donna

K. Wells, was the architect of Virginia's statewide criminal-justice plan and the Governor's Comprehensive Crime Prevention Plan for Virginia.

Morris's criminal-justice experience spans two decades. Morris served previously as Deputy Secretary of Public Safety, Chairman of the Parole Board, and Director of the Department of Criminal Justice Services. He was twice elected Commonwealth's Attorney (state prosecutor) for the combined jurisdictions of Harrisonburg and Rockingham County, Virginia.

A frequent lecturer on criminal justice and public-safety topics, Morris also serves as a faculty member of Virginia Commonwealth University's Commonwealth Educational Policy Institute.

Morris graduated with distinction from the Virginia Military Institute, where he is a member of the Board of Visitors, and received his Juris Doctorate degree from the William & Mary Marshall-Wythe School of Law.